The Low-Cholesterol Vegan Diet: Food Lists and Cookbook

Delicious, Easy-to-Make Plant-Based Recipes for a Healthy Heart, Quick Weight Loss, and Reduced Risk of Stroke

Kaitlyn Jones, RDN

FOREWORD

In today's world of diet trends and conflicting advice, finding a plan that truly works can feel overwhelming. This book changes that by offering science-backed principles and practical steps, making healthy living both accessible and sustainable.

Unlike many other diet guides, this one doesn't promise quick fixes. Instead, it empowers you to make informed choices that align with your unique goals and lifestyle.

Kaitlyn Jones, RDN, brings a wealth of knowledge and a deep passion for helping others succeed, offering not just recipes and tips but a shift in mindset—viewing food as an ally in your journey to wellness.

If you're just beginning your path to better health or looking to refine your approach, this book will guide you with clarity, empathy, and actionable advice. Remember, progress, not perfection, is the key to success. As you turn these pages, you'll find inspiration and tools to take control of your health, one choice at a time.

Dr. James Brady, MD

Board-Certified Nutrition Specialist and Wellness Advocate

COPYRIGHT PAGE

Copyright © 2025 by Kaitlyn Jones, RDN

All rights reserved. No part of this publication may be reproduced, distributed, or transmitted in any form or by any means, including photocopying, recording, or other electronic or mechanical methods, without the prior written permission of the publisher, except in the case of brief quotations embodied in critical reviews or articles.

Published by

Bluescript

5001 JT Memorial Hwy, Charles City, Virginia, 23871

Disclaimer: The information in this book is for educational purposes only. The author and publisher are not liable for any adverse effects or consequences resulting from the use of the information in this book. Always consult with a healthcare provider before making significant changes to your diet or lifestyle.

TABLE OF CONTENTS

FOREWORD 2
COPYRIGHT PAGE 4
TABLE OF CONTENTS 5
All You Need to Know About Veganism 1
   Benefits of a Vegan, Low-Cholesterol Diet 18
Essential Plant-Based Nutrition Basics 22
   Fiber-full for Cholesterol Management 32
Recipes for Low Cholesterol Vegan Breakfast Diet 36
   Plant-Based Jackfruit Carnitas Tacos Recipe 36
   Oven-Roasted Purple Cauliflower Salad Recipe 38
   Vegan Tofu "Chorizo" Quesadilla Recipe 39
   Cucumber Avocado Salsa Recipe 41
   Crispy Stuffed Aloo Tikki Recipe 42
   Poblano Potato Breakfast Hash Recipe 45
   Vegan Chewy Oatmeal Cookie Recipe 47
   Fluffy, Almost-Eggy Chickpea Scramble Recipe 48
   Air Fryer Veggie-Stuffed Cabbage Rolls Recipe 50
   No-Bake Vegan Raspberry Matcha Bars Recipe 52
   Vegan Watermelon "Tuna" Bowl Recipe 54
   Vibrant Tropical Smoothie Bowl Recipe 55

Charred Avocado Hand Rolls Recipe 56
Recipes for Low Cholesterol Vegan Lunch Diet 58
   Vegan Hearts Of Palm "Lobster" Roll Recipe 58
   Smoky And Creamy Sweet Potato Dip Recipe 59
   Baked Panelle Sandwich Recipe 60
   Smoky Jackfruit Chili Recipe 62
   Vegetable Chow Mein Noodle Soup Recipe 64
   Chilled Beet And Tomato Soup Recipe 65
   Silky Pumpkin And Tofu Curry Recipe 67
   Garden Art Vegetable Focaccia Recipe 68
   Cabbage And Lentil Curry Soup Recipe 70
   Kale, Chickpea, And Dukkah Salad Recipe 72
   Tofu Burgers With Grilled Pineapple Salsa Recipe . 74
   Grilled Mediterranean Tofu Skewers With Green Olive Relish Recipe 75
   Summer Turnip Salad With Lemon-Herb Dressing Recipe 77
   Fajita Pasta With Cilantro Lime Sauce Recipe 78
Recipes for Low Cholesterol Vegan Dinner Diet 81
   Shredded Brussels Sprouts Tacos With Charred Corn Salsa Recipe 81
   Red Lentil Falafel Pita Sandwich Recipe 82
   Polos Curry (Sri Lankan Jackfruit Coconut Curry) Recipe 84

Baked Ratatouille Casserole With Garam Masala Recipe 85

Classic Kung Pao Tofu Recipe 87

Spaghetti And Zucchini Noodle Vegan Garden Pasta Recipe 89

Twice-Fried Salt And Pepper Tofu Recipe 90

Silken Tofu And Soba Noodle Salad Recipe 92

Sigeumchi Namul-Inspired Vegan Quiche Recipe .. 93

Super Springy Vegetable Soup Recipe 95

Cajun Tofu Bowl With Avocado-Maple Dressing Recipe 97

Ethiopian-Inspired Berbere Split Peas Recipe 99

Spicy Sriracha Tofu Spring Rolls Recipe 101

Recipes for Low Cholesterol Vegan Snacks and Desserts Diet 103

Vegan Chocolate-Covered Digestive Biscuits (Vegan McVities) 103

Homemade Wheat Thins Recipe 105

Vegan Spinach and Artichoke Dip Recipe 108

Potato Chips With Mushrooms, Lemon, and Thyme Recipe 111

Za'atar (Thyme-, Sesame-, and Sumac-Spiced) Popcorn Recipe 112

Cheese-Free Sweet Potato "Quesadillas" Recipe 113

Oven-Roasted Tomato Bruschetta Recipe 115

Oven-Dried Grapes (a.k.a. Raisins) Recipe 116

Avocado Toast With Radishes, Baby Peas, and Fresh Herbs Recipe 117

The Best Applesauce 118

Easy Vegan Crispy Tofu Spring Rolls 120

Korean Fried Cauliflower (Vegan) Recipe 121

Low Cholesterol Vegan Hummus 123

Making This Diet Work for You 126

Kaitlyn Jones, RDN

All You Need to Know About Veganism

According to the Vegan Society, the term "vegan" was coined back in 1944 by a small group of vegetarians who broke away from the Leicester Vegetarian Society in England to form the Vegan Society.

In addition to refraining from eating meat, they chose not to consume dairy, eggs, or any other products of animal origin.

The term "vegan" was chosen from the combination of the first and last letters of "vegetarian." By 1949, the first definition of veganism had been born. It has changed slightly over the years to become what it is known as today.

According to the latest definition from the Vegan Society, veganism is "a philosophy and way of living which seeks to exclude — as far as is possible and practicable — all forms of exploitation of, and cruelty to, animals for food, clothing, or any other purposes."

Kaitlyn Jones, RDN

Many people use the term "vegan" to refer exclusively to diet. However, by this latest definition, veganism extends beyond eating a plant-based diet.

Those who identify as vegans typically aim to exclude animal exploitation or cruelty in all aspects of their lives, including the clothes they wear, the cosmetics they use, and the leisure activities they take part in.

As a result, many vegans avoid purchasing wool coats, leather furniture, or down pillows and comforters. They may also opt to visit animal sanctuaries instead of going to zoos, the circus, or animal petting farms.

History

Although the vegan diet was defined early on in The Vegan Society's beginnings in 1944, by Donald Watson and our founding members.It was as late as 1949 before Leslie J Cross pointed out that the society lacked a definition of veganism. He suggested "[t]he principle of the emancipation of animals from exploitation by man". This is later clarified as "to seek an end to the use of animals by man for food, commodities, work, hunting, vivisection, and by all other uses involving exploitation of animal life by man".

The society was first registered as a charity in August 1964 but its assets were later transferred to a new charity when it also became a limited company in December 1979. The definition of veganism and the charitable objects of the society were amended and refined over the years. By winter 1988 the current definition was in use - although the phrasing has changed slightly over the years.

Why do people go vegan?

People generally choose to avoid animal products for one or more of the following reasons.

Ethics

Ethical vegans strongly believe that all creatures have a right to life and freedom.

They view all animals as conscious beings that, just like humans, wish to avoid pain and suffering.

Because of this, ethical vegans are opposed to killing an animal in order to eat its flesh or wear its fur or skin.

Vegans are also opposed to the psychological and physical stress that animals may endure as a result of modern farming practices — for instance, the small pens or cages that animals typically live in and rarely leave between their birth and slaughter.

However, for ethical vegans, this sentiment extends beyond the cruelty of modern farming practices.

That's because vegans are opposed to consuming products that heavily rely on the killing of other animals — especially because alternatives are available.

This includes the slaughter of calves that are considered surplus in the dairy industry, or the culling of 1-day-old male chicks that is common in egg production.

Moreover, ethical vegans generally believe that animals' milk, eggs, honey, silk, and wool are not for humans to exploit, regardless of the living conditions afforded to the exploited animals.

This is why ethical vegans remain opposed to drinking an animal's milk, eating its eggs, or wearing its wool, even in cases where the animals are free-roaming or pasture-fed.

Health

Some people choose a vegan diet for its potential health benefits.

Diets high in meat — especially red meat — have been linked to cancer, heart disease, and type 2 diabetes.

On the other hand, plant-based diets have been linked to a lower risk of developing or prematurely dying from these diseases.

Lowering your intake of animal products in favor of more plant-based options may also improve your digestion and reduce your risk of Alzheimer's disease.

A vegan diet can also help minimize the side effects linked to the antibiotics and hormones used in modern animal agriculture.

Finally, vegan diets appear to be especially effective at helping people lose unwanted weight. Several studies link a vegan diet to a lower likelihood of obesity.

However, if you're on a vegan diet, you may consume less of certain nutrients. That's why planning is especially important.

Consider speaking with a healthcare professional, such as a doctor or registered dietitian, to plan a vegan diet that will help you get the nutrients you need.

Vegan diets tend to be low in these nutrients:

- vitamin B12

- vitamin D

- calcium

- zinc

- iodine

- selenium

People on vegan diets sometimes take supplements to provide nutrients they may not get enough of in their diet.

Environment

People may also choose to avoid animal products in an attempt to limit their environmental impact.

Kaitlyn Jones, RDN

According to recent data, animal agriculture heavily contributes to greenhouse gas emissions (GHGEs), which cause climate change.

Meat eaters are thought to be responsible for 2–2.5 times more GHGEs than people following a vegan diet. This number is based on self-reported dietary patterns in the U.K.

Ruminant animals, such as cattle, sheep, and goats, appear to emit the largest amount of greenhouse gases per gram of protein they deliver. Therefore, diets that reduce or totally eliminate dairy also produce significantly fewer GHGEs.

One study suggests that a vegetarian diet produces 33% fewer GHGEs than a meat-containing standard American diet offering the same amount of calories.

A vegan diet has an even smaller environmental impact, producing about 53% fewer GHGEs than a calorie-matched meat-containing diet.

A large proportion of the plant protein currently being produced is used to feed animals rather than humans. Because of this, production of an animal-heavy diet requires use of more of the earth's resources than production of a plant-based diet.

For instance, producing animal protein requires 6–17 times more land than the same amount of soybean protein.

Animal protein also requires, on average, 2–3 times more water, depending on factors such as the season and annual fluctuations in rainfall.

Because of all of these factors, experts estimate that, if nothing changes, our food system will likely exceed our planet's resources by the year 2050. Switching over to a vegan diet may be one way to delay this outcome.

Types of veganism

It's important to note that vegan doesn't necessarily equal healthy.

The quality of a vegan diet depends on the foods that make it up. Thus, some vegan diets can have many health benefits, while others may not be beneficial for your health.

Here are a few subcategories of vegan diet that I've come across in my clinical practice over the last couple of years:

- **Dietary vegans.** Often used interchangeably with "plant-based eaters," this term refers to those who avoid animal products in their diet but continue to use them in other products, such as clothing and cosmetics.

- **Whole-food vegans.** These individuals favor a diet rich in whole foods, such as fruits, vegetables, whole grains, legumes, nuts, and seeds.

- **"Junk-food" vegans.** Some people rely heavily on processed vegan foods such as vegan meats, fries, frozen dinners, and desserts, including Oreo cookies and nondairy ice cream.

- **Raw-food vegans.** This group eats only foods that are raw or cooked at temperatures below 118°F (48°C).

- **Low fat raw-food vegans.** Also known as fruitarians, this subset limits high fat foods such as nuts, avocados, and coconuts, instead relying mainly on fruit. They may occasionally eat small amounts of other plants.

Whole-food vegan diets tend to offer excellent health benefits. If you're interested in trying a vegan diet, consider speaking with a healthcare professional to find the right diet for you.

What do vegans eat?

Here are some essential foods people on a vegan diet tend to eat and avoid.

Foods that vegans eat

Avoiding animal products doesn't restrict you to eating salads and tofu alone. There's a wide variety of delicious foods you can eat on a vegan diet.

Here are a few ideas:

- **Beans, peas, and lentils:** such as red, brown, or green lentils; chickpeas; split peas; black-eyed peas; black beans; white beans; and kidney beans

- **Soy products:** such as fortified soy milk, soybeans, and products made from them, such as tofu, tempeh, and natto

- **Nuts:** such as peanuts, almonds, cashews, and their butters

- **Seeds:** such as sunflower seeds, sesame seeds, and their butters, as well as flaxseed, hemp seeds, and chia seeds

- **Whole grains:** such as quinoa, whole wheat, whole oats, and whole grain brown or wild rice, as well as products made from these foods, such as whole grain bread, crackers, and pasta

- **Starchy vegetables:** such as potatoes, sweet potatoes, corn, squash, beets, and turnips

- **Nonstarchy vegetables:** such as broccoli, cabbage, asparagus, radishes, and leafy greens; these may be raw, frozen, canned, dried, or pureed

- **Fruit:** such as apples, pears, bananas, berries, mango, pineapple, oranges, and tangerines; these may be purchased fresh, frozen, canned, dried, or pureed

- **Other plant-based foods:** such as algae, nutritional yeast, fortified plant milks and yogurts, and maple syrup

There's a good chance that many of the dishes you currently enjoy either already are vegan or can be made vegan with a few simple adjustments.

For instance, you can swap meat-based main dishes for meals containing beans, peas, lentils, tofu, tempeh, nuts, or seeds.

What's more, you can replace dairy products with plant milks, scrambled eggs with scrambled tofu, honey with plant-based sweeteners like molasses or maple syrup, and raw eggs with flaxseed or chia seeds.

You can also choose from the ever-growing selection of ready-made vegan products, including vegan meats, vegan cheeses, and vegan desserts.

Just keep in mind that these may be highly processed. So while they are fine to eat in moderation, they should not make up the bulk of a healthy vegan diet.

Foods that vegans avoid

Vegans avoid all foods of animal origin. These include:

- **Meat and fish:** such as beef, chicken, duck, fish, and shellfish

- **Eggs:** whole eggs and foods that contain them, such as bakery products

- **Dairy:** milk, cheese, butter, and cream, as well as foods made using these ingredients

- **Other animal-derived ingredients:** such as honey, albumin, casein, carmine, gelatin, pepsin, shellac, isinglass, and whey

Checking food labels is generally the best way to determine whether a food contains animal-derived ingredients. Many vegan foods are now also labeled as such, making it easier to recognize them when you're shopping.

Vegan vs. Vegetarian: What's the Difference?

What is a vegetarian diet?

According to the Vegetarian society, a vegetarian is someone who does not eat any meat, poultry, game, fish, shellfish, or by-products of animal slaughter.

Vegetarian diets contain various levels of fruits, vegetables, grains, pulses, nuts, and seeds.

The inclusion of dairy, honey, and eggs depends on the type of diet you follow.

The most common types of vegetarians include:

- **Lacto-ovo vegetarians:** vegetarians who avoid all animal flesh, but do consume dairy and egg products

- **Lacto vegetarians:** vegetarians who avoid animal flesh and eggs, but do consume dairy products

- **Ovo vegetarians:** vegetarians who avoid all animal products except eggs

- **Vegans:** vegetarians who avoid all animal and animal-derived products

People who do not eat meat or poultry but do consume fish are considered pescatarians, whereas part-time vegetarians are often referred to as flexitarians.

Although they're sometimes considered vegetarians, pescatarians and flexitarians do eat animal flesh. So, they do not technically fall under the definition of vegetarianism.

What is a vegan diet?

A vegan diet can be viewed as the strictest form of vegetarianism.

Veganism is currently defined by the Vegan Society as a way of living that attempts to exclude all forms of animal exploitation and cruelty as much as possible.

This includes exploitation for food and any other purpose.

So, a vegan diet not only excludes animal flesh, but also dairy, eggs, and other ingredients that come from animals. These include:

- gelatin
- honey
- carmine
- pepsin
- shellac
- albumin
- whey
- casein
- some forms of vitamin D3

Vegetarians and vegans often avoid eating animal products for similar reasons. The largest difference is the degree to which they consider animal products acceptable.

For instance, both vegans and vegetarians may exclude meat from their diets for health or environmental reasons.

Vegans also choose to avoid all animal by-products because they believe this has the largest impact on their health and the environment.

In terms of ethics, vegetarians are opposed to killing animals for food, but generally consider it acceptable to consume animal by-products such as milk and eggs, as long as the animals are kept in adequate conditions.

On the other hand, vegans believe that animals have a right to be free from human use, whether it's for food, clothing, science, or entertainment.

As a result, they seek to avoid all animal by-products, regardless of the conditions in which animals are bred or housed.

The desire to avoid all forms of animal exploitation is why vegans choose to forgo dairy and eggs — products that many vegetarians have no problem consuming.

Nutrition considerations for vegetarian and vegan diets

Research shows vegetarian and vegan diets tend to be low in saturated fat and cholesterol.

They also tend to contain high amounts of vitamins, minerals, fiber, and healthy plant compounds.

What's more, both diets contain a high amount of nutrient-dense foods. These may include fruit, vegetables, whole grains, nuts, seeds, and soy products.

On the other hand, poorly planned vegetarian and vegan diets could result in low intakes of some nutrients, particularly iron, calcium, zinc, and vitamin D.

Both diets also tend to contain limited amounts of vitamin B_{12} and long-chain omega-3 fatty acids, although levels of these nutrients are generally lower in vegans than vegetarians.

While vegetarian and vegan diets tend to lean heavily on fruits, legumes, and vegetables, some items might be diary- and meat-free but are still:

• highly processed

• high in added sugars

• cooked using methods that can add excess fat

Cookies, french fries, candies, and even nut-based ice creams may fall into the vegan and vegetarian category yet still contain refined carbohydrates, are highly processed, are high in added sugar, or are deep fried.

These items should be consumed in moderation.

Which is healthier?

According to a report from the Academy of Nutrition and Dietetics, both vegetarian and vegan diets can be considered appropriate for all stages of life, as long as the diet is planned well.

An insufficient intake of nutrients such as omega-3 fatty acids, calcium, and vitamins D and B12 can negatively impact various aspects of health, including mental and physical health.

Both vegetarians and vegans may have lower intakes of these nutrients. However, studies show that vegetarians tend to consume slightly more calcium and vitamin B12 than vegans.

Nonetheless, both vegetarians and vegans should pay special attention to nutrition strategies meant to increase the absorption of nutrients from plant foods.

It may also be necessary to consume fortified foods and supplements, especially for nutrients such as iron, calcium, omega-3, and vitamins D and B12.

Vegetarians and vegans should strongly consider:

- analyzing their daily nutrient intake
- getting their blood nutrient levels measured
- taking supplements accordingly

The few studies directly comparing vegetarian to vegan diets report that vegans may have a somewhat lower risk of developing type 2 diabetes, heart disease, and various types of cancer than vegetarians.

That said, most studies so far have been observational in nature. This means that it's impossible to say exactly which aspect of the vegan diet produces these effects and to confirm that diet is the only determining factor.

Veganism is about more than what you eat

Although vegetarians and vegans may choose to avoid animal products for similar purposes, this choice often extends beyond diet for vegans.

In fact, veganism is often considered a lifestyle strongly anchored in animal rights.

For this reason, many vegans also avoid purchasing clothing items containing silk, wool, leather, or suede.

What's more, many vegans boycott companies that test on animals and purchase only cosmetics that are free of animal by-products.

People known as "ethical vegans" also tend to steer clear of circuses, zoos, rodeos, horse races, and any other activities involving the use of animals for entertainment.

Finally, many environmentalists adopt a vegan diet for its reduced impact on the earth's resources and the benefits it has against climate change.

Kaitlyn Jones, RDN

Benefits of a Vegan, Low-Cholesterol Diet

1. Improved Heart Health

Your heart works hard every single day, and what you eat can make or break its performance. A vegan diet is a game-changer for heart health because it's naturally free from dietary cholesterol—cholesterol only comes from animal products. By cutting out meat, dairy, and eggs, you're giving your heart a break.

But it doesn't stop there. Many plant-based foods, like oats, beans, and nuts, actively help reduce LDL cholesterol (the "bad" kind that clogs arteries). The fiber in these foods acts like a broom, sweeping cholesterol out of your body before it has a chance to cause trouble. Over time, this can lower your risk of heart disease, strokes, and high blood pressure.

2. Weight Management Made Easier

Let's face it—managing weight can feel like a constant battle. But switching to a vegan diet often makes it simpler. Plant-based foods are generally lower in calories and saturated fats compared to animal products. Think about it: a hearty lentil soup will fill you up and fuel your body with nutrients, while a greasy burger does the opposite.

Vegan meals, especially when based on whole foods like fruits, veggies, and grains, are nutrient-dense. That means they're packed with vitamins and minerals but not heavy on calories, so you stay satisfied without overeating. Whether you're looking to shed a few pounds or just maintain a healthy weight, a vegan, low-cholesterol diet helps you stay on track without the guilt.

3. Lower Risk of Chronic Diseases

When you eat plant-based, you're not just feeding yourself—you're protecting your future. Research shows that vegan diets can lower the risk of chronic conditions like type 2 diabetes, certain cancers, and high blood pressure. The secret lies in plants' natural ability to fight inflammation and neutralize harmful free radicals with antioxidants.

For instance, fruits like berries and leafy greens are packed with compounds that protect your cells from damage. Meanwhile, the healthy fats in avocados and nuts keep your blood vessels flexible, reducing strain on your heart. By eating this way, you're not just avoiding illness—you're building a foundation for a long, healthy life.

4. Better Digestive Health

Imagine waking up every day feeling light and energized instead of bloated and sluggish. That's what a vegan diet can do for your digestion. The fiber in plant-based foods is a powerhouse for your gut—it keeps things moving smoothly, preventing constipation and reducing the risk of digestive issues like diverticulitis.

Fiber also feeds the good bacteria in your gut, creating a balanced microbiome. A healthy gut doesn't just mean good digestion; it's linked to stronger immunity, better mood, and even improved brain function. So when you fill your plate with fruits, veggies, and legumes, you're doing your whole body a favor.

5. Making a Positive Impact on the Planet

Every meal you eat is a chance to make a difference—not just for your body, but for the world around you. Vegan diets are far kinder to the environment. Animal farming is one of the leading causes of deforestation, water pollution, and greenhouse gas emissions. By eating plant-based, you're choosing a lifestyle that uses fewer resources and helps preserve the planet for future generations.

And let's not forget the ethical side of things. For many, going vegan is a way to take a stand against animal cruelty. Every plant-based meal is a choice to protect animals and embrace compassion.

6. Boosted Energy and Mental Clarity

One of the first things people notice when they switch to a vegan, low-cholesterol diet is how much better they feel—inside and out. Without the heavy load of saturated fats weighing you down, your body uses energy more efficiently. Whole, plant-based foods like bananas, sweet potatoes, and quinoa provide steady, long-lasting fuel.

This steady energy isn't just physical. Many people report sharper focus, improved mood, and even better sleep after adopting a vegan lifestyle. When you're feeding your body the nutrients it craves, it rewards you with vitality that keeps you thriving.

Kaitlyn Jones, RDN

2
Essential Plant-Based Nutrition Basics

Protein is an essential macronutrient building block for various bodily tissues, including muscles, enzymes, hormones, and immune components. One of the most common misconceptions about vegan diets is the belief that they lack sufficient protein.

However, with proper planning, vegans can easily obtain all the protein they need. An abundance of plant-based protein sources can rival or even surpass the protein content of animal-derived products.

Legumes such as lentils, chickpeas, and black beans are excellent protein sources, as are tofu, tempeh, and edamame.

Additionally, whole grains like quinoa, brown rice, oats, nuts and seeds like almonds, chia seeds, and pumpkin seeds are rich in protein.

It is crucial to vary protein sources to ensure you receive a diverse array of amino acids, the building blocks of protein.

Kaitlyn Jones, RDN

Combining different plant-based protein sources in your meals can create complete protein profiles that provide all the essential amino acids your body needs.

Calculating your protein needs depends on various factors, including age, gender, activity level, and individual goals.

While the general recommended dietary allowance for protein is 0.8 grams per kilogram of body weight, active individuals or those seeking muscle gain may require more.

Consulting a registered dietitian can help you determine your specific protein needs and develop a personalised meal plan to meet them effectively.

Iron

Iron is a vital mineral in transporting oxygen throughout the body.

It is especially crucial for maintaining healthy blood and preventing iron-deficiency anaemia.

Plant-based sources of iron, known as non-haem iron, may have lower absorption rates compared to heme iron found in animal products. However, several strategies to optimise iron absorption on a vegan diet exist.

Dark leafy greens like spinach, kale, and Swiss chard are excellent sources of iron, as are beans and lentils.

Additionally, different dried fruits will be a good source of iron, such as apricots and raisins.

To enhance iron absorption, pair iron-rich foods with vitamin C-rich foods, as vitamin C aids in absorbing non-haem iron.

For example, adding bell peppers to a spinach salad or squeezing lemon juice over lentils can significantly boost iron absorption.

Conversely, it is advisable to avoid consuming calcium-rich foods, such as dairy alternatives or fortified plant-based milks, at the same time as iron-rich foods, as calcium can hinder iron absorption.

Vitamin B12

Vitamin B12 is a water-soluble vitamin essential for nerve function, DNA synthesis, and the formation of red blood cells.

While some plant-based foods like nutritional yeast and fortified plant milk may contain vitamin B12, they may not provide sufficient amounts for meeting daily requirements.

As a result, vegans need to consider vitamin B12 supplementation.

Vitamin B12 supplements are available in various forms, including tablets, sublingual (under-the-tongue) drops, and fortified foods.

Regularly monitoring your vitamin B12 levels and consulting with a nutritionist can help ensure you maintain adequate levels of this essential nutrient.

Omega-3 Fatty Acids

Omega-3 fatty acids are polyunsaturated fats crucial in brain health, heart health, and reducing inflammation.

While animal products like fatty fish are well-known sources of omega-3 fatty acids, vegans can obtain them from plant-based sources.

The primary plant-based omega-3 fatty acid is alpha-linolenic acid (ALA) in flaxseeds, chia seeds, hemp seeds, and walnuts.

The body can convert ALA into long-chain omega-3 fatty acids, eicosapentaenoic acid (EPA), and docosahexaenoic acid (DHA).

However, this conversion process could be more efficient.

To ensure an adequate intake of EPA and DHA, consider incorporating algae-based supplements derived from microalgae and provide a direct source of these beneficial fatty acids.

Vegan-friendly supplements are available in various forms, including capsules and oils.

They can help bridge the gap in omega-3 fatty acid intake for vegans.

The Significance of Balanced Macronutrient Intake

A well-balanced vegan diet should meet nutrient needs and ensure a proper balance of macronutrients: carbohydrates, proteins, and fats.

Each macronutrient plays a distinct role in supporting bodily functions and overall health.

Carbohydrates are the body's primary energy source, and they can be found in various plant-based foods like grains, fruits, vegetables, and legumes.

Complex carbohydrates, such as those found in whole grains, provide sustained energy and are valuable to any vegan diet.

As discussed earlier, protein is essential for tissue repair and growth, and it is vital to include diverse plant-based protein sources to ensure a complete range of amino acids.

Healthy fats, such as monounsaturated and polyunsaturated fats, are crucial for brain health, hormone regulation, and overall well-being. Sources of healthy fats for vegans include avocados, nuts and seeds.

Vegan Sources of Healthy Fats, Carbohydrates, and Proteins

Kaitlyn Jones, RDN

Emphasising whole, nutrient-dense foods is key to obtaining a balanced macronutrient intake on a vegan diet.

Incorporating a wide variety of fruits, vegetables, whole grains, legumes, nuts, and seeds into your meals provides an array of essential nutrients and helps maintain a proper macronutrient balance.

Avocados, for instance, are a rich source of healthy fats and contain fibre and essential vitamins and minerals.

A simple avocado toast or adding sliced avocados to salads can provide a nutritious boost to your diet.

Quinoa, often called a "complete protein" because it contains all nine essential amino acids, is a fantastic grain to incorporate into your meals. Pair it with colourful vegetables and a flavourful dressing for a nutritious vegan meal.

Nuts and seeds offer a wealth of healthy fats, protein, and micronutrients. Sprinkle chia seeds on your morning smoothie bowl or snack on a handful of almonds for a quick energy boost and a dose of essential nutrients.

Tips for Creating Well-Rounded Meals

To craft well-rounded and nourishing vegan meals, consider using the following tips:

1. **Aim for various colours on your plate**: Different-coloured fruits and vegetables signify the presence of different antioxidants and phytonutrients, providing a spectrum of health benefits.

2. **Incorporate whole grains**: opt for whole grains like brown rice, quinoa, and oats, which offer more fibre, vitamins, and minerals than refined grains.

3. **Combine complementary proteins**: As mentioned earlier, combining different plant-based protein sources can create complete protein profiles. For instance, pairing beans with rice or tofu with broccoli ensures you receive all essential amino acids.

4. **Remember healthy fats**: Add avocados, nuts, and seeds to your meals to increase healthy fat intake. Fats absorb fat-soluble vitamins, such as A, D, E, and K.

5. **Experiment with herbs and spices**: Enhance the flavour of your dishes with herbs and spices, which add taste and bring their health benefits.

Vitamin D

Vitamin D, often called the "sunshine vitamin," is crucial for bone health, immune function, and overall well-being.

While the sun is a natural source of vitamin D, it may be challenging for vegans, especially those living in regions with limited sunlight, to obtain adequate amounts solely from sunlight exposure.

Vegan-friendly sources of vitamin D include fortified plant-based milk alternatives and certain types of mushrooms exposed to UV light. However, relying solely on dietary sources may not provide sufficient vitamin D.

As a result, supplementation may be necessary, especially during the winter months or if you have limited sun exposure.

Zinc

Zinc is essential in immune function, cell division, and wound healing. Plant-based sources of zinc include legumes, nuts, seeds, whole grains, and fortified cereals.

However, phytates, compounds found in whole grains, legumes, and nuts, can hinder zinc absorption from plant-based foods.

To improve zinc absorption, soaking, sprouting, or fermenting these foods can help reduce phytate content.

Additionally, pairing zinc-rich foods with sources of vitamin C may enhance absorption.

Vitamin C

Vitamin C is a potent antioxidant that supports the immune system, aids collagen formation, and enhances iron absorption.

Fortunately, vitamin C is abundant in various plant-based foods.

Citrus fruits, such as oranges, grapefruits, and lemons, are well-known sources of vitamin C.

Other excellent sources include strawberries, kiwis, bell peppers, broccoli, and Brussels sprouts.

To retain the maximum vitamin C content in your foods, consider using gentle cooking methods like steaming or eating fruits and vegetables raw.

Omega-3 Fatty Acids

While I discussed omega-3 fatty acids in the previous section, it is essential to reiterate their importance as powerful antioxidants that combat inflammation and promote heart and brain health.

In addition to their role as omega-3 sources, flaxseeds and chia seeds contain lignans, plant compounds with antioxidant properties.

Including these seeds in your diet contributes to your overall antioxidant intake.

Iron

Though I already touched on iron in the previous section, it is essential to highlight the importance of vitamin C in enhancing iron absorption. Vitamin C-rich foods, such as citrus fruits, strawberries, and leafy greens, can significantly improve the absorption of non-haem iron from plant-based sources.

Moreover, avoiding consuming calcium-rich foods alongside iron-rich meals can further enhance iron absorption.

Therefore, when planning meals, try to balance the inclusion of iron, vitamin C, and calcium sources throughout the day.

Other Essential Micronutrients

While we've covered several essential micronutrients, such as vitamin B12, iron, vitamin D, zinc, and vitamin C, it is crucial to remember that a well-rounded vegan diet can provide most, if not all, of the essential micronutrients your body requires.

By focusing on whole, nutrient-dense plant-based foods and ensuring a diverse diet, you will naturally consume various vitamins, minerals, and antioxidants that promote overall health and well-being.

Kaitlyn Jones, RDN

Fiber-full for Cholesterol Management

The American Heart Association and the FDA recommend that we all eat at least 25 grams of dietary fiber per day. But what is it, how do we know how much we're eating, and where did that number come from, anyway?

What are the types of fiber?

Dietary fiber is a good carbohydrate, also known as roughage, found in plant foods (not supplements). There are two kinds, soluble or insoluble, and both are really good for us. Soluble fiber becomes a thick gel in our intestines, which slows digestion (which keeps blood sugars from spiking) and traps fats so they can't all be absorbed (which lowers cholesterol levels). Sources of soluble fiber include oatmeal, beans, lentils, and many fruits. Insoluble fiber helps keep our stools soft and regular, always a good thing! Sources of insoluble fiber include whole grains, beans, lentils, and most vegetables. Both soluble and insoluble fiber make us feel full, which helps us to eat less.

Why is fiber so good for us?

But fiber does so, so much more. In a recent research study published in The Lancet, investigators pooled the results from 243 studies looking at health effects of dietary fiber.

They excluded any studies about fiber supplements — this was all about fiber from food. They ended up with data from over 4,600 people, and found a very strong relationship between higher dietary fiber intake and better health outcomes. Basically, intake of at least 25 grams of food fiber a day is associated with a lower weight, blood pressure, blood sugars, cholesterol, as well as lower risk of developing (or dying from) diabetes, heart disease, strokes, and breast or colon cancer.

Study results were extremely consistent, and the dose-response curve was very linear, meaning the more fiber, the better the outcomes. This makes us believe the results are very real and not due to some other factor related to study participants' diet or lifestyle.

Consuming good carbs means more daily fiber

Unfortunately, most of us are consuming fewer than 20 grams of fiber per day. I know many people who shy away from the carbs in whole grains, beans, and fruit, thus missing out on all that healthy fiber. But here's the deal: there's good carbs and bad carbs, and whole grains, beans, and vegetables are all good, folks. It's the quality of the carb that counts. Worried about gassy effects? In the short term, start low and use simethicone (a common, gentle anti-gas medication) as needed. Your body will become accustomed over time, and the effects will diminish.

Fiber-packed meals are easy

Let's put together a very simple yet flexible meal using boiled red lentils, store-bought or homemade hummus, whole-wheat wraps, and a simple salad made with mixed greens, tomatoes, and cucumbers dressed with only lemon juice and olive oil. This meal is so easy and healthy, and it can be served to guests or packed up for lunch at the work desk. This meal has half the recommended daily fiber and almost 20 grams of protein, plus calcium, iron, and potassium.

Mediterranean-Style Heart-Healthy High-Fiber Buffet

Many of these ingredients can be purchased inexpensively or prepared super-quickly, and no one will know you weren't cooking all day.

Cooked and seasoned red lentils (1 cup raw lentils to 3 cups water, bring to a boil and simmer for 15 minutes, then sprinkle with sea salt and lemon juice. Add chopped fresh herbs too, if you like. Serve hot or cold.)

Very simple salad (mixed greens, sliced cherry tomatoes, and chopped cucumber, dressed in extra virgin olive oil, lemon juice, sea salt, and black pepper. Toss it all up and serve.)

1 container hummus (or you can make your own)

Whole-wheat wraps

Optional: kalamata olives, artichoke hearts, sundried tomatoes, baba ganouj, or other Mediterranean goodies, low-salt versions preferred.

There are many resources available to guide you on healthy high-fiber food choices. Basically, consuming fruits, veggies, beans and legumes, and nuts and seeds regularly will ensure that you get at least 25 grams of fiber every day!

Kaitlyn Jones, RDN

3

Recipes for Low Cholesterol Vegan Breakfast Diet

Plant-Based Jackfruit Carnitas Tacos Recipe

Ingredients

- 3 (14.1-ounce) cans jackfruit in brine
- 2 oranges
- 2 tablespoons avocado oil
- ½ diced onion
- 3 minced garlic cloves
- 1 ½ teaspoons salt, divided
- ¼ teaspoon pepper
- 2 teaspoons cumin, divided
- 1 teaspoon chili powder
- 1 teaspoon oregano
- 2 bay leaves
- 2 tablespoons coconut sugar
- 5 tablespoons lime juice, divided
- 1 cup vegetable broth
- 1 avocado
- 1 cup cilantro
- 8 small soft tortillas

- 1 diced tomato

Optional Ingredients

- chopped cilantro
- sliced avocado

Cooking Directions

1. Remove the jackfruit from the can and rinse it well with cold water
2. Cut off the point of each jackfruit piece and discard.
3. With your hands, shred the jackfruit and set it aside.
4. Juice the oranges.
5. Add the oil to a large pan and bring the heat to medium.
6. Add the onion, garlic, ½ teaspoon of salt, and pepper and cook for 5 minutes.
7. Preheat the oven to 400 F.
8. Add the jackfruit, 1 teaspoon of cumin, chili powder, oregano, bay leaves, sugar, orange juice, 2 tablespoons of lime juice, and broth to the frying pan. Cook on medium heat for about 20 minutes stirring frequently till most of the liquid has cooked off.
9. Remove the bay leaves and spread the jackfruit on a sheet pan. Bake for 30 minutes, stirring halfway.
10. While it's cooking combine the avocado, cilantro, remaining teaspoon of cumin, ½ cup water, remaining 3 tablespoons lime juice, and remaining teaspoon of salt to a

blender and blend until smooth.

11. Warm up the tortillas.

12. To assemble, layer the cooked jackfruit, tomatoes, and sauce into the tortillas. Garnish with avocado slices, and cilantro if desired.

Oven-Roasted Purple Cauliflower Salad Recipe

Ingredients

- 1 head purple cauliflower, cut into florets
- Cooking spray
- 2 teaspoons za'atar, divided
- 1½ teaspoons salt, divided
- 3 tablespoons olive oil
- 2 tablespoons apple cider vinegar
- ½ teaspoon grainy mustard
- ½ teaspoon garlic powder
- ¼ teaspoon pepper
- 6 cups mixed greens
- 1 Honeycrisp apple
- 1 avocado
- ¼ cup Marcona almonds
- ¼ cup pomegranate seeds

Cooking Directions

1. Preheat the oven to 400 F

2. Line a baking sheet with parchment paper

3. Spread the cauliflower florets on the baking sheet.

4. Spray with cooking spray, 1 teaspoon of za'atar, and ½ teaspoon salt. Bake for 20 minutes. Leave for 10 minutes to cool.

5. In the meantime, make the dressing by combining the oil, vinegar, mustard, garlic powder, remaining salt, remaining za'atar and pepper.

6. Core and chop the apple and peel, pit, and chop the avocado.

7. Add the greens to a bowl along with the cooked cauliflower, apple, avocado, almonds, and pomegranate seeds.

8. Add the dressing, toss, and serve.

Vegan Tofu "Chorizo" Quesadilla Recipe

Ingredients

- 1 cup raw cashews, unsalted
- 4 tablespoons avocado oil, divided
- 3 tablespoons soy sauce
- 1 tablespoon + 1 teaspoon apple cider vinegar, divided
- 2 teaspoons chili powder
- 1 ½ teaspoons smoked paprika

- 1 ½ teaspoons garlic granules, divided
- 1 teaspoon onion granules, divided
- 1 teaspoon oregano
- 1 teaspoon cumin
- ½ teaspoon coriander
- 1 ½ (16-ounce) blocks of super firm tofu
- ½ cup water
- 3 tablespoons cooked and mashed sweet potato or pumpkin puree
- 2 tablespoons diced canned green chiles
- 2 tablespoons nutritional yeast
- 1 tablespoons tapioca starch
- 2 tablespoons lemon juice
- ½ teaspoon salt
- ¼ teaspoon dry mustard
- 3 large flour tortillas

Optional Ingredients

- cilantro, to serve
- salsa, to serve

Cooking Directions

1. Soak the cashews in boiling water for 30 minutes.
2. Preheat the oven to 400 F.
3. Prepare a sheet pan with parchment paper.
4. In a large bowl mix 2 tablespoons avocado oil, soy sauce, 1 tablespoon vinegar, chili powder, smoked paprika, 1 teaspoon garlic granules, ½

teaspoon onion granules, oregano, cumin, and coriander.

5. With your hands, crumble the tofu into the bowl.

6. Mix to coat all of the tofu.

7. Spread the tofu out on the sheet pan and bake for 30 minutes stirring twice.

8. Meanwhile, rinse and drain the cashews.

9. Add them to a blender with the remaining vinegar, remaining garlic granules, remaining onion granules, water, mashed sweet potato, green chiles, nutritional yeast, tapioca starch, lemon juice, salt, and dry mustard.

10. Blend until smooth

11. Spread ⅓ of the tofu chorizo on half of each tortilla, then top with ⅓ of the cashew cheese and fold over.

12. Add ½ tablespoon of avocado oil to a skillet and bring the heat to medium-high.

13. Lay in the folded quesadilla and sear on each side for 3-4 minutes. Repeat with other tortillas.

14. Top with optional chopped cilantro, slice, and serve.

Cucumber Avocado Salsa Recipe

Ingredients

- 1 clove garlic, grated
- 2 tablespoons olive oil

Kaitlyn Jones, RDN

- Juice of 1 lime
- 1 teaspoon salt
- 2 cups diced cucumber
- 2 cups diced avocado
- 1 cup corn kernels
- ½ cup diced red onion
- ½ cup finely chopped cilantro

Cooking Directions

1. In a large bowl, whisk together the garlic, olive oil, lime juice, and salt.
2. Add the cucumber, avocado, corn, onion, and cilantro and mix until well combined.
3. Serve with tortilla chips or as desired.

Crispy Stuffed Aloo Tikki Recipe

Ingredients

- For the potato mixture
- 1 ¼ pounds medium russet potatoes, unpeeled
- ½ teaspoon ground cayenne
- 1 teaspoon finely chopped green chile
- ½ teaspoon garam masala
- ½ teaspoon ground coriander
- 1 tablespoon grated ginger
- 1 tablespoon lemon juice
- 1 tablespoon finely chopped cilantro
- ¾ teaspoon salt

Kaitlyn Jones, RDN

- ¼ cup breadcrumbs
- 1 tablespoon cornstarch
- For the pea stuffing
- 1 cup frozen peas
- ¼ teaspoon ground cayenne
- 1 teaspoon finely chopped green chile
- ½ teaspoon ground coriander
- ¼ teaspoon ground cumin
- 1 tablespoon grated ginger
- ½ teaspoon lemon juice
- 2 tablespoons finely chopped cilantro
- ¼ teaspoon salt
- For frying
- Oil for frying

Optional Ingredients

- Chutney for serving

Cooking Directions

1. Place the potatoes in a medium pot and cover them with about 1 inch of water.

2. Bring the water to a gentle boil and let the potatoes cook for 15-20 minutes until fork tender.

3. When the potatoes are finished, drain them and place them on a dish or cooling rack. Let them cool until they can be easily handled.

4. While the potatoes are cooling, make the pea stuffing. Bring a small pot of water to a boil, add the peas, and boil

for 2-4 minutes until tender.

5. Drain the peas, place them in a medium bowl, and roughly mash them with a fork.

6. Add the pea stuffing ingredients -- cayenne, green chile, coriander, cumin, ginger, lemon juice, cilantro, and salt -- and mix well. Taste and adjust for salt or other seasonings. Set aside.

7. Peel the potatoes with a paring knife.

8. Place the potatoes in a mixing bowl and mash them with a fork or potato masher until smooth. Set aside to cool completely, about 15 minutes.

9. Add the potato mixture ingredients -- cayenne, green chili, garam masala, coriander, ginger, lemon juice, cilantro, salt, breadcrumbs, and cornstarch -- and mix well. Taste and adjust for salt or other seasonings. The dough shouldn't be too dry or too sticky.

10. Shape the potato mixture into 6 balls of equal size. The dough may crack, especially if it is too dry. You can repair the cracks by pressing the dough back together, moistening the area with a very small amount of water if needed.

11. Shape each ball into a cup shape with a depressed center.

12. Spoon about 2 tablespoons of filling into each potato cup.

13. Push the sides of the potato cups up to cover the stuffing and seal the tops.

14. Gently roll the potato balls to smooth them out and then flatten them into patties.

15. Heat a shallow layer of frying oil in a frying pan until hot.

16. Place the patties in the oil in batches and fry, undisturbed, for 4-5 minutes until the underside is golden and crispy.

17. Flip the patties and fry for an additional 4-5 minutes until the other side is golden and crispy. Remove from the heat and place on paper towels to absorb extra moisture.

18. Serve immediately with chutney, if desired.

Poblano Potato Breakfast Hash Recipe

Ingredients

- 3 tablespoons avocado oil
- 2 potatoes, peeled and diced
- 2 poblano peppers, diced
- 1 red onion, diced, divided
- 2 garlic cloves, minced
- 1 red bell pepper, diced

- 1 (15-ounce) can black beans
- 1 teaspoon salt, divided
- ½ teaspoon cumin
- ½ teaspoon smoked paprika
- ¼ teaspoon pepper
- 2 diced tomatoes
- ½ cup chopped cilantro
- ½ tablespoon diced jalapeño
- Juice of 1 lime

Optional Ingredients

- sliced avocado for serving

Cooking Directions

1. Heat the oil in a skillet over medium-high heat.
2. Add the potatoes and cook for about 15 minutes, until they are beginning to get tender.
3. Add the poblanos, all but 2 tablespoons of red onion, garlic, red pepper, black beans, ½ teaspoon salt, cumin, smoked paprika, and pepper. Stir and cook for about 10 minutes or until the peppers are soft.
4. Meanwhile, combine the tomatoes, cilantro, remaining red onion, jalapeño, lime juice, and remaining salt to make pico de gallo.
5. Plate the breakfast hash with pico de gallo and optional avocado before serving.

Kaitlyn Jones, RDN

Vegan Chewy Oatmeal Cookie Recipe

Ingredients

- 1 tablespoon ground flax seed
- 3 tablespoons water
- ½ cup melted coconut oil
- ½ cup coconut sugar
- ¼ cup maple syrup
- 1 teaspoon vanilla extract
- 1 cup all-purpose flour
- ½ teaspoon baking soda
- 1 teaspoon cinnamon
- ¼ teaspoon salt
- Pinch of ground cloves
- 1 ½ cups rolled oats

Cooking Directions

1. In a small bowl combine the ground flax seed with 3 tablespoons of water and let sit for 10 minutes.
2. In a large bowl combine the coconut oil, coconut sugar, maple syrup, vanilla extract, and flax mixture.
3. In a medium bowl mix together the flour, baking soda, cinnamon, salt, and cloves.
4. Fold in the oats.
5. Add the dry ingredients to the wet ingredients.
6. Cover and refrigerate for 30 minutes.
7. Preheat the oven to 350 F.

8. Prepare a baking sheet with parchment paper.

9. Form 12 cookies with about 2 tablespoons of the mixture for each cookie, and lay out on the prepared baking sheet.

10. Bake for 10 minutes and let them sit on the baking sheet for 10 minutes after baking.

11. Transfer the cookies to a cooling rack for 10 more minutes before serving.

Fluffy, Almost-Eggy Chickpea Scramble Recipe

Ingredients

- 1 (15.5-ounce) can chickpeas
- 2 tablespoons aquafaba from the chickpea can
- 1 tablespoon avocado oil
- ½ cup diced onion
- 3 garlic cloves, minced
- 1 diced red bell pepper
- 1 tablespoon chickpea flour
- 1 tablespoon nutritional yeast
- 1 teaspoon salt
- ½ teaspoon kala namak
- ¼ teaspoon smoked paprika
- ¼ teaspoon turmeric
- ¼ teaspoon pepper
- ¼ cup vegetable broth
- 1 diced plum tomato

- 1 cup chopped spinach

Optional Ingredients

- cilantro
- avocado
- jalapenos
- toast

Cooking Directions

1. Drain the chickpeas over a bowl to collect the aquafaba.
2. Measure out 2 tablespoons and set aside.
3. Mash the chickpeas to a chunky texture with a fork, a food chopper, or a food processor. Be careful not to over-process.
4. Add the oil to a frying pan and bring the heat to medium.
5. Add the onion, garlic, and red pepper and saute for 5 minutes stirring frequently.
6. In a small bowl combine the aquafaba with the chickpea flour, stir with a small whisk to make a slurry, and then set it aside.
7. Add the mashed chickpeas, nutritional yeast, salt, kala namak, smoked paprika, turmeric, pepper, and broth. Stir to combine.
8. Add the chickpea flour slurry and reduce the heat to a simmer. Cook for 5 minutes.
9. Add the tomato and spinach and cook on simmer for about 3 minutes until the spinach wilts.

10. Serve on toast topped with optional fresh cilantro, avocado, and jalapeño, and serve.

Air Fryer Veggie-Stuffed Cabbage Rolls Recipe

Ingredients

- ¾ cup diced mushrooms
- ½ cup diced red bell pepper
- ½ cup shredded carrots
- ½ cup edamame
- ¼ cup diced onion
- 2 garlic cloves, minced
- 1 teaspoon + 2 teaspoons sesame oil, divided
- ½ teaspoon cumin
- ½ teaspoon coriander
- ½ teaspoon garam masala
- ¼ teaspoon + ¼ teaspoon powdered ginger, divided
- ¼ teaspoon turmeric
- 1 head green cabbage
- cup cooked rice
- 1 teaspoon avocado oil
- 2 tablespoons soy sauce
- 1 tablespoon rice vinegar
- ¼ teaspoon red chili flakes

Optional Ingredients

- sesame seeds

Cooking Directions

1. Add the mushroom, red pepper, carrots,

edamame, onion, garlic, 1 teaspoon sesame oil, cumin, coriander, garam masala, ¼ teaspoon ginger, and the turmeric to an oven safe dish that will fit in your air fryer. Stir to combine.

2. Cook in the air fryer for 10 minutes at 400 F.

3. Add the cooked rice to the vegetable mixture.

4. Cut the core off of the cabbage and peel gently to separate the leaves. You'll need 10-12 leaves.

5. With a paring knife, trim down the stem on each cabbage leaf.

6. Place the leaves in boiling water for 4 minutes.

7. Place the cabbage leaves vertically in front of you with the core end closest, and add 2-3 tablespoons of the vegetable/rice mixture.

8. Fold in the sides of the cabbage and wrap up into a tight roll and place in the air fryer basket. Repeat until you've used up each cabbage leaf and all of the filling.

9. Brush each roll with avocado oil.

10. Cook for 12 minutes at 350 F. You may have to work in batches depending on the size of your air fryer.

11. While the rolls are cooking, combine the remaining sesame oil, soy sauce, vinegar, remaining ginger, and red chili flakes.

12. Serve the rolls with the sauce and optional sesame seeds.

No-Bake Vegan Raspberry Matcha Bars Recipe

Ingredients

- 2 cups Medjool dates
- 1 ½ cup raw cashews, divided
- 1 cup walnuts
- ½ cup slivered almonds
- ¼ cup rolled oats
- 2 tablespoons + 2 teaspoons coconut oil, divided
- ½ cup coconut cream
- ½ cup maple syrup, divided
- 2 tablespoons matcha
- 1 teaspoon vanilla
- 1 tablespoon lemon juice
- 1 pinch salt
- 1 ½ cups frozen raspberries
- 2 tablespoons chia seeds

Cooking Directions

1. Add the dates to a bowl and cover with hot water. Let sit for 15 minutes.
2. Add the cashews to a small bowl and cover with boiling water. Let sit for 15 minutes, then drain.
3. Remove and discard the pits from the dates.

4. Prepare a 9x9-inch baking dish by lining it with parchment paper.

5. Add the dates, ½ cup drained cashews, walnuts, almonds, oats, and 2 teaspoons coconut oil to a food processor. Pulse until well blended.

6. Press the date mixture into the prepared baking dish and place in the fridge for 30 minutes to set.

7. Add the remaining soaked cashews, coconut cream, ¼ cup maple syrup, matcha, vanilla, remaining coconut oil, lemon juice, and salt to the food processor and blend until smooth.

8. Pour this layer over the crust layer and put into the freezer for 30 minutes.

9. Heat the frozen raspberries and remaining ¼ cup maple syrup in a small pot over medium heat for 10 minutes, stirring frequently.

10. Remove from the heat and add the chia seeds. Stir and let sit for 15 minutes.

11. Spread the raspberry chia jam over the matcha layer and let sit in the freezer for 2 hours.

12. Use a sharp knife to cut the bars into 9 squares.

13. Serve, or store the bars in the freezer for later.

Kaitlyn Jones, RDN

Vegan Watermelon "Tuna" Bowl Recipe

Ingredients

- 4 cups cubed seedless watermelon
- 3 tablespoons soy sauce
- 2 tablespoons rice vinegar
- 1 tablespoon sriracha
- 2 teaspoons sesame oil
- 1 tablespoon dulse granules
- 1 garlic clove, crushed
- ½ teaspoon powdered ginger
- ½ tablespoon sesame seeds
- 4 cups chopped romaine
- 1 cup carrot ribbons or shredded carrots
- 1 cup shelled edamame
- 1 cup cooked rice
- ½ English cucumber, sliced
- 2 radishes, sliced
- ½ avocado, sliced
- ½ mango, sliced

Optional Ingredients

- Lime wedges

Cooking Directions

1. Preheat the oven to 350 F.
2. Arrange the watermelon on a baking sheet and cook for 45 minutes, then cool for 30 minutes.
3. In a small bowl, combine the soy

sauce, vinegar, sriracha, sesame oil, dulse granules, garlic, ginger, and sesame seeds.

4. Add the watermelon to the bowl and toss gently.

5. Cover and marinate for 1 hour.

6. Distribute the lettuce between two bowls, then add the marinated watermelon, edamame, cooked rice, carrots, cucumber, radishes, avocado, and mango.

7. Garnish with optional lime wedges, and serve.

Vibrant Tropical Smoothie Bowl Recipe

Ingredients

- 2 passion fruits
- 1 cup fresh pineapple, cubed
- 1 cup frozen banana chunks
- 1 cup frozen mango
- ¼ cup coconut milk
- 1 kiwi, sliced
- 1 star fruit, sliced
- ¼ cup fresh mango, cubed
- ½ dragon fruit, chopped or balled
- ¼ cup blueberries
- 2 tablespoons coconut flakes
- 4 golden berries

Cooking Directions

1. Prepare the passion fruits by halving each one and scooping out the pulp.

2. Add the pineapple, frozen banana, frozen mango, passion fruit pulp, and coconut milk to a food processor.

3. Blend the mixture for 20 to 30 seconds until it has the consistency of soft-serve ice cream.

4. Transfer the smoothie mixture to a serving bowl.

5. Adorn the smoothie bowl(s) with the kiwi slices, star fruit, cubed mango, dragon fruit, blueberries, golden berries, and coconut flakes.

6. Serve immediately.

Charred Avocado Hand Rolls Recipe

Ingredients

- 1 large Hass avocado, pitted
- 1 cup yuzu ponzu with dashi
- 2 sheets toasted standard-size nori, cut in half width-wise
- 1 ½ cups prepared and seasoned sushi rice
- ½ Persian cucumber, cut into matchsticks
- ⅓ cup sprouts or micro greens

Optional Ingredients

- Wasabi, pickled ginger, and soy sauce, for serving

Cooking Directions

1. Remove the avocado from its skin and cut it into 8 segments.

2. Place the avocado on a rimmed baking sheet.

3. Using a blow torch, lightly char each piece of avocado. Alternatively, use a grill or grill pan to add char to the avocado halves before slicing.

4. Carefully place the avocado segments in a bowl with the yuzu dashi, using a spoon to coat.

5. Let the avocado marinate for about 10 minutes.

6. To assemble the rolls, place a sheet of nori shiny side down.

7. Scoop about ¼ cup of the rice onto the left side of the rectangle at an angle toward the bottom center of the piece.

8. Top the rice with 2 segments of avocado.

9. Add a few matchsticks of cucumber and a sprinkle of sprouts.

10. Fold the bottom-left corner of the nori over the filling and roll to form a cone, using a wet finger to seal the final edge.

11. Repeat with the remaining rolls and serve immediately.

Kaitlyn Jones, RDN

4

Recipes for Low Cholesterol Vegan Lunch Diet

Vegan Hearts Of Palm "Lobster" Roll Recipe

Ingredients

- 3 (14-ounce) cans hearts of palm cylinders
- 2 diced celery stalks
- 1 tablespoon chopped fresh dill + more for topping
- 1 tablespoon chopped chives
- 1 teaspoon chopped capers
- ½ cup vegan mayonnaise
- 2 teaspoons Old Bay seasoning
- 2 tablespoons lemon juice
- ½ teaspoon sriracha
- ¼ teaspoon pepper
- ⅛ teaspoon salt
- 4 sub-style rolls

Optional Ingredients

- paprika for serving

Cooking Directions

1. Drain the hearts of palm and rinse them well.

2. Roughly chop the hearts of palm and add them to a large bowl.

3. Add the celery, dill, chives, and capers. Stir gently to combine.

4. In a medium bowl combine the mayonnaise, Old Bay seasoning, lemon juice, sriracha, pepper, and salt.

5. Toss the mayo mixture with the hearts of palm mixture.

6. Cover and chill in the fridge for a minimum of 30 minutes.

7. Fill the rolls with the hearts of palm lobster.

8. Top with fresh dill and paprika, if desired, and serve.

Smoky And Creamy Sweet Potato Dip Recipe

Ingredients

- 2 medium sweet potatoes
- 3 tablespoons tahini
- 1 teaspoon Dijon mustard
- 1 tablespoon lime juice
- 1 teaspoon salt
- ½ teaspoon cumin
- ½ teaspoon garlic granules
- ¼ teaspoon cayenne pepper

- ¼ teaspoon smoked paprika

Optional Ingredients

- Chopped cilantro, for serving

Cooking Directions

1. Preheat the oven to 400 F.
2. Line a sheet pan with parchment paper
3. Poke the sweet potatoes with a fork in 6–8 spots.
4. Place the potatoes on the sheet pan and bake for 45 minutes, until very soft.
5. Let them cool on the sheet pan for 15 minutes.
6. Cut the sweet potatoes open and scoop the flesh out into a bowl.
7. Add the tahini, Dijon, lime juice, salt, cumin, garlic granules, cayenne pepper, and smoked paprika. Stir to combine.
8. Top with chopped cilantro, if desired, and serve.

Baked Panelle Sandwich Recipe

Ingredients

- 1 ¾ cups chickpea flour
- 1 teaspoon salt
- 3 cups + 3 tablespoons water
- 1 tablespoon minced parsley
- Olive oil, for greasing/drizzling

- 1 lemon
- 4 soft sesame seed rolls

Cooking Directions

1. Place the chickpea flour and salt in a medium saucepan and whisk well.

2. Slowly pour the water in a little at a time, whisking continuously. Don't pour all of the water in at once or it will be hard to get the clumps out.

3. Heat the pan on medium, stirring continuously so that the flour doesn't stick to the bottom. Once the mixture comes to a boil, lower it to a simmer and stir continuously for about 10 minutes, until thickened. It should be compact and fall off the spoon extremely slowly.

4. Remove the pan from the heat and stir in the parsley.

5. Line a large baking sheet with parchment paper.

6. Pour the mixture onto the baking sheet and, using a knife or a spatula, spread it into an even layer about ¼ inch high. Adjust the edges to make them straight so that no scraps are wasted later. Set aside to cool completely, about 1 hour.

7. Preheat the oven to 400 F.

8. Cut even shapes (rectangles, squares, or triangles) out of the cooled chickpea

mixture with a knife or cookie cutter and place them on a parchment paper–lined baking sheet. Use two sheets, if necessary.

9. Drizzle a little olive oil on top of the panelle.

10. Bake for 30–35 minutes, until the underside and edges are lightly browned.

11. Squeeze a little lemon juice on the panelle before serving hot or at room temperature on soft sesame seed buns.

Smoky Jackfruit Chili Recipe

Ingredients

- 2 (15-ounce) cans young jackfruit in brine
- 1 tablespoon avocado oil
- 1 diced onion
- 3 minced garlic cloves
- 1 chopped red bell pepper
- 1 diced jalapeño pepper, seeds discarded
- 1 diced Serrano pepper, seeds discarded
- 2 tablespoons tomato paste
- 2 teaspoons cumin

Kaitlyn Jones, RDN

- 1 teaspoon chili powder
- 1 teaspoon coriander
- 1 teaspoon oregano
- 1 teaspoon smoked paprika
- 1 teaspoon salt
- ¼ teaspoon black pepper
- 1 can black beans, rinsed and drained
- 1 can pinto beans, rinsed and drained
- 1 (15-ounce) can fire-roasted tomatoes
- 2 cups vegetable broth
- 1 tablespoon lime juice

Optional Ingredients

- Chopped red onion, for serving
- Chopped cilantro, for serving
- Sliced avocado, for serving
- Sliced jalapeño, for serving

Cooking Directions

1. Drain and rinse the jackfruit.
2. Cut the hard tip off each jackfruit piece and discard.
3. Shred the jackfruit with your hands.
4. Add the oil to a large pot and bring the heat to medium-high.
5. Add the onion, garlic, red pepper, jalapeño, and Serrano pepper and saute for 5 minutes.

6. Next, add the tomato paste, cumin, chili powder, coriander, oregano, smoked paprika, salt, and pepper and stir for 2 minutes on medium heat.

7. Add the shredded jackfruit, black beans, pinto beans, fire-roasted tomatoes, and broth to the pot, reduce heat to low, and cook for 1 hour. Stir the mixture occasionally.

8. Stir in the lime juice.

9. Serve the chili with optional red onion, cilantro, avocado, and jalapeño.

Vegetable Chow Mein Noodle Soup Recipe

Ingredients

- 1 tablespoon sesame oil
- 2 garlic cloves, minced
- 2 carrots, diced
- 1 red bell pepper, sliced
- ½ small cabbage, chopped
- 3 cups chopped broccoli
- 4 cups vegetable broth
- 3 tablespoons soy sauce
- 1 tablespoon hoisin sauce
- 1 tablespoon Shaoxing wine
- 1 teaspoon sriracha

- ½ teaspoon salt
- 8 ounces uncooked chow mein noodles
- ½ cup bean sprouts
- 3 scallions, chopped

Cooking Directions

1. Add the oil to a large soup pot and bring the heat to medium.
2. Add the garlic, carrots, and red pepper, and saute for 8 minutes.
3. Add the cabbage, broccoli, broth, soy sauce, hoisin sauce, Shaoxing wine, sriracha, and salt. Bring to a boil, then cook on medium for 8 minutes.
4. Add the noodles, 3 cups water, and bean sprouts. Cook on medium-high for 10 minutes, or until the noodles are done.
5. Top with scallions, and serve.

Chilled Beet And Tomato Soup Recipe

Ingredients

- 4 medium red beets, greens and stems discarded
- 1 tablespoon avocado oil
- 1 teaspoon salt, divided
- ¼ teaspoon pepper, divided
- 1 English cucumber, diced
- 1 red bell pepper, diced

- 3 large beefsteak tomatoes, diced
- ¼ cup diced red onion
- 2 minced garlic cloves
- 4 cups tomato juice
- Juice of ½ lemon
- 2 tablespoons apple cider vinegar
- ½ cup chopped parsley

Cooking Directions

1. Preheat the oven to 400 F.
2. Line a sheet pan with parchment paper.
3. Pierce the beets all over with a fork.
4. Place the beets on the sheet pan, brush them with oil, and sprinkle with ¼ teaspoon salt and ⅛ teaspoon pepper. Bake for 45 minutes to 1 hour.
5. In the meantime, combine the cucumber, red pepper, tomatoes, red onion, garlic, remaining salt, and remaining pepper in a large bowl or pot and stir well.
6. Add the tomato juice, lemon juice, and vinegar.
7. When the beets are done baking and slightly cooled, peel and discard the skin.
8. Dice the beets.
9. Add the beets to the pot with the other ingredients, cover, and chill for 1 hour.
10. Top with chopped parsley and serve.

Kaitlyn Jones, RDN

Silky Pumpkin And Tofu Curry Recipe

Ingredients

- ¼ cup tomato paste
- 1 crushed garlic clove
- 1 teaspoon grated ginger
- 1 tablespoon chili powder
- 1 teaspoon cumin
- 1 teaspoon coriander
- 1 tablespoon soy sauce
- 1 tablespoon + 1 teaspoon lime juice, divided
- ½ teaspoon turmeric
- 1 cup canned pumpkin puree
- 1 tablespoon avocado oil
- 1 diced yellow onion
- 1 diced red bell pepper
- 1 (16-ounce) package super firm tofu, cubed
- 1 (13.5-ounce) can full fat coconut milk
- 1 cup vegetable broth
- 1 tablespoon coconut sugar
- 1 teaspoon salt
- ¼ teaspoon pepper
- 4 cups packed baby spinach

Optional Ingredients

- cooked rice
- chopped cilantro

Cooking Directions

1. Make a red curry paste by combining the tomato paste, garlic, ginger, chili powder,

cumin, coriander, soy sauce, 1 tablespoon lime juice, and turmeric in a medium pot.

2. Cook on low heat, stirring occasionally for 5 minutes.

3. Add the pumpkin puree and simmer for 5 minutes.

4. Add the oil to a large pot over medium-high heat.

5. Saute the onion and bell pepper for 8 minutes.

6. Add the cubed tofu and cook for 15 minutes, stirring frequently until the edges start to brown.

7. Add the pumpkin and red curry paste mixture, coconut milk, broth, sugar, salt, and pepper. Bring to a boil, then cook on low for 10 minutes.

8. Stir in spinach and remaining lime juice and cook for 3 minutes or until the spinach has wilted.

9. Top the tofu pumpkin curry with cilantro if desired and optionally serve with rice.

Garden Art Vegetable Focaccia Recipe

Ingredients

- For the focaccia dough

- 1 (¼-ounce) package instant yeast

- 2 teaspoons granulated sugar

- 4 ½ cups bread flour (or all-purpose)

Kaitlyn Jones, RDN

- 1 tablespoon kosher salt, divided
- 6 tablespoons olive oil, divided
- ¼ teaspoon freshly cracked black pepper
- For the vegetable topping
- ½ small red onion, thinly sliced
- 3 spears fresh asparagus, trimmed
- 1 green onion, thinly sliced
- 6 multicolored cherry tomatoes, halved
- 3 multicolored mini sweet peppers, stemmed and thinly sliced
- ¼ cup fresh flat-leaf parsley leaves
- ¼ cup fresh rosemary sprigs
- 4 pitted black olives, thinly sliced

Cooking Directions

1. In the bowl of a stand mixer fitted with a hook attachment, combine 2 cups water with the yeast, sugar, flour, 2 ½ teaspoons salt, and 2 tablespoons olive oil.

2. Mix on medium speed for 6 to 8 minutes, until all of the ingredients are thoroughly combined into a sticky dough.

3. Cover and set aside for 30 minutes.

4. Uncover the dough. Wet your hands and then lift and fold the dough onto itself three or four times.

5. Cover and set aside for another 30 minutes.
6. Repeat steps 4 and 5 twice.
7. Spread 2 tablespoons olive oil into a 9x13-inch baking pan.
8. Pour the dough into the pan and coat with the remaining 2 tablespoons olive oil.
9. Gently stretch the dough to coat the bottom of the pan, taking care not to deflate any air bubbles along the way.
10. Cover and let rise for 45 minutes.
11. Preheat the oven to 400 F.
12. Unwrap the dough and use your fingertips to dimple the surface.
13. Decoratively top the dough with the vegetables. Sprinkle with the remaining ½ teaspoon salt and the pepper.
14. Bake for 30 to 35 minutes, or until golden brown.
15. Let stand in pan for 10 minutes, and then transfer to a cutting board.
16. Cut the bread into portions and serve warm or at room temperature.

Cabbage And Lentil Curry Soup Recipe

Ingredients

- 1 tablespoon avocado oil

Kaitlyn Jones, RDN

- 1 teaspoon cumin seeds
- 1 teaspoon mustard seeds
- 1 yellow onion, diced
- 2 garlic cloves, minced
- 1 teaspoon grated ginger
- 1 teaspoon ground coriander
- 1 teaspoon ground cumin
- 1 teaspoon turmeric powder
- ½ teaspoon garam masala
- ¼ teaspoon chili powder
- 1 carrot, diced
- 1 red bell pepper, diced
- 5 cups chopped green cabbage
- 1 cup dried brown lentils
- 1 (14 ½-ounce) can diced tomatoes
- 6 cups vegetable broth
- 1 teaspoon salt
- ¼ teaspoon black pepper
- ½ lemon, juiced

Optional Ingredients

- Chopped cilantro

Cooking Directions

1. Add the oil to a large soup pot and bring the heat to medium.
2. Add the cumin seeds and mustard seeds and stir for 1 minute.
3. Now, add the onion, garlic, and ginger and

cook for about 5 minutes.

4. Add the coriander, ground cumin, turmeric, garam masala, and chili powder. Stir for 1 minute to coat the aromatics.

5. Now, add the carrot and red pepper and cook for about 5 minutes.

6. Add the cabbage and stir for 1 minute.

7. Add the lentils, tomatoes, broth, salt, and black pepper.

8. Bring to a boil, cover, then simmer for 20–25 minutes, or until the lentils are tender.

9. Add the lemon juice, optionally top with chopped cilantro, and serve.

Kale, Chickpea, And Dukkah Salad Recipe

Ingredients

- 2 preserved lemons, separated
- 1 large garlic clove
- 3 tablespoons pomegranate molasses
- 2 tablespoons lemon juice
- ½ teaspoon Dijon mustard
- ¼ teaspoon black pepper
- ¾ cup olive oil
- 7 ounces kale
- 1 tablespoon toasted sesame seed oil
- 2 large ripe avocados

- 1 (14-ounce) can chickpeas, drained
- ¼ cup fresh cilantro, chopped
- ¼ cup pomegranate seeds
- 2 tablespoons dukkah

Cooking Directions

1. To make the dressing, add 1 preserved lemon, the garlic clove, pomegranate molasses, lemon juice, Dijon mustard, black pepper, and olive oil to a blender.
2. Blend the ingredients on high for 20 to 30 seconds until smooth.
3. Set the dressing aside.
4. Wash and remove any woody stalks from the kale.
5. Drizzle the kale with the toasted sesame oil and then massage the leaves for a few minutes until they start to soften and wilt.
6. Slice the avocado into chunks.
7. Add the kale, chickpeas, avocado, cilantro, and salad dressing to a bowl.
8. Toss well to coat everything with the dressing and transfer the salad to a large serving plate.
9. Slice the remaining preserved lemon and add it on top of the salad along with pomegranate seeds and dukkah.
10. Serve the kale and chickpea salad.

Kaitlyn Jones, RDN

Tofu Burgers With Grilled Pineapple Salsa Recipe

Ingredients

- 1 (14-ounce) package extra-firm tofu, drained and pressed
- ¼ cup soy sauce
- 2 tablespoons rice vinegar
- 2 cloves garlic, minced
- 1 teaspoon grated ginger
- 2 (1-inch thick) slices of pineapple, cored and peeled
- ½ red onion, diced
- 1 jalapeño, seeded and diced
- ¼ cup chopped cilantro
- 1 tablespoon lime juice
- 4 buns
- 1 ripe avocado, sliced

Cooking Directions

1. Slice the tofu into 4 equal patties.
2. In a small bowl, whisk together the soy sauce, vinegar, garlic, and ginger.
3. Place tofu in a shallow dish and cover with marinade, turning to coat both sides. Marinate for at least 30 minutes, flipping once.
4. Preheat a grill pan to medium-high heat.
5. Grill the pineapple slices until charred, about 2-3 minutes per side. Remove from heat and let cool slightly.

6. Dice the grilled pineapple and transfer it to a bowl with the diced onion, jalapeño, cilantro, and lime juice. Toss to combine. Set aside.

7. Grill the marinated tofu patties on medium-high heat for 4-5 minutes per side, until they're heated through and grill marks appear.

8. Preheat the oven to broil.

9. Toast the buns for 2 minutes in an oven set to broil.

10. Brush the remaining marinade from the tofu over the bottom of the bun.

11. Assemble the burger: top the tofu with pineapple cilantro salsa and slices of avocado, and cover with the second bun half.

12. Serve the tofu burgers with more salsa on the side.

Grilled Mediterranean Tofu Skewers With Green Olive Relish Recipe

Ingredients

- ½ cup olive oil + 3 tablespoons, divided
- zest and juice of 1 ½ lemons
- 1 tablespoon minced shallot
- 3 crushed garlic cloves, divided
- 1 tablespoon maple syrup

- 2 teaspoons Dijon mustard
- 1 tablespoon + 1 teaspoon minced fresh dill, divided
- 1 tablespoon minced chives
- ½ teaspoon salt
- ¼ teaspoon pepper
- 1 (16-ounce) package of extra firm tofu, pressed for 10 minutes
- 1 cup heirloom cherry tomatoes
- 1 thickly sliced zucchini
- 1 red pepper, cut into chunks
- 1 red onion, cut into thick chunks
- 1 (15-ounce) can whole artichoke hearts, drained
- 1 cup pitted castelvetrano olives
- 1 cup pitted medium green ripe olives
- 1 tablespoon capers
- 3 tablespoons fresh basil leaves

Cooking Directions

1. In a small bowl combine ½ cup olive oil, zest and juice of 1 lemon, shallots, 1 crushed garlic clove, maple syrup, Dijon mustard, 1 tablespoon dill, chives, salt, and pepper.

2. Put the tofu, cherry tomatoes, zucchini, red pepper, red onion, and artichoke hearts into a large bowl and toss with marinade.

3. Cover and marinate in the fridge for 1 hour.

4. Add the olives, capers, remaining olive oil, remaining garlic, remaining lemon zest and juice, remaining dill, and basil to a food processor and pulse a few times to get a chunky mixture. Set aside.

5. When the vegetables and tofu are almost done marinating, preheat the grill to medium-high.

6. Thread the tofu and vegetables on to 4 metal skewers and place on the grill.

7. Cook for 12 minutes on each side or until the vegetables and tofu are browned.

8. Serve with green olive relish, remaining marinade, and optional rice.

Summer Turnip Salad With Lemon-Herb Dressing Recipe

Ingredients

- 3 turnips
- ¼ cup sliced red onion
- 1 cup sliced English cucumber
- 1 cup halved grape tomatoes
- 1 cup chopped Italian parsley
- 1 lemon
- 3 tablespoons olive oil
- 1 tablespoon minced shallot
- 1 crushed garlic clove
- 1 tablespoon maple syrup

- 2 teaspoons Dijon mustard
- 1 tablespoon minced dill
- 1 tablespoon minced chives
- ½ teaspoon salt
- ¼ teaspoon pepper

Cooking Directions

1. Peel the turnips and cut off the ends.
2. Thinly slice the peeled turnips by hand or with a mandoline.
3. In a large bowl combine the sliced turnips, cucumber, tomatoes, and parsley.
4. Zest and juice the lemon.
5. In a small bowl combine the olive oil, lemon zest and juice, shallot, garlic, maple syrup, mustard, dill, and chives.
6. Toss the salad with dressing and serve.

Fajita Pasta With Cilantro Lime Sauce Recipe

Ingredients

- 8 ounces ziti pasta
- 1 tablespoon avocado oil
- 1 red bell pepper, sliced
- 1 green bell pepper, sliced
- 1 yellow bell pepper, sliced
- 1 poblano pepper, sliced

Kaitlyn Jones, RDN

- 1 red onion, sliced
- 5 garlic cloves, minced and divided
- 1 teaspoon chili powder
- 1 teaspoon ground cumin
- 1 teaspoon salt, divided
- ¼ teaspoon smoked paprika
- ¼ teaspoon garlic powder
- ¼ teaspoon onion powder
- ¼ teaspoon dried oregano
- ¼ teaspoon black pepper
- 1 cup cilantro
- ¼ cup olive oil

- 2 tablespoons lime juice
- 1 teaspoon maple syrup
- ¼ teaspoon coriander

Optional Ingredients

- Chopped cilantro
- Lime slices

Cooking Directions

1. Bring a large pot of water to a boil.
2. Cook the pasta according to the package Cooking Directions. Drain and set aside.
3. Add the avocado oil to a large skillet and bring the heat to medium-high.
4. Add the peppers, onion, 3 garlic cloves, chili powder, cumin,

½ teaspoon salt, paprika, garlic powder, onion powder, oregano, and pepper. Saute for 10 minutes, stirring frequently.

5. Add the cilantro, olive oil, lime juice, maple syrup, remaining salt, coriander, remaining garlic, and 2 tablespoons of water to a small food processor. Blend until smooth.

6. Add the pasta and sauce to the skillet.

7. Stir together, then serve.

Kaitlyn Jones, RDN

5

Recipes for Low Cholesterol Vegan Dinner Diet

Shredded Brussels Sprouts Tacos With Charred Corn Salsa Recipe

Ingredients

- 2 tablespoons avocado oil, divided
- 3 cups corn
- 1 diced jalapeño
- 1 cup black beans
- 1 diced tomato
- ½ cup fresh cilantro
- ¼ cup diced red onion
- 1 diced avocado
- 4 tablespoons lime juice, divided
- 1 teaspoon salt, divided
- 4 cups shredded or shaved Brussels sprouts
- 1 teaspoon chili powder
- 1 teaspoon cumin
- ¼ teaspoon garlic granules
- ¼ teaspoon onion granules

- ¼ teaspoon oregano
- ¼ teaspoon paprika
- 12 soft taco shells

Cooking Directions

1. Add 1 tablespoon of oil to a cast iron skillet over high heat.
2. Add the corn and cook for about 10 minutes stirring frequently, until browned.
3. Remove the corn from the skillet and add to a bowl along with the jalapeño, black beans, tomato, cilantro, red onion, avocado, 2 tablespoons lime juice, and ½ teaspoon salt.
4. Add the remaining oil back to the same skillet used earlier and bring the heat to medium.
5. Drop in the Brussels sprouts and the remaining lime juice, chili powder, cumin, remaining salt, garlic granules, onion granules, oregano, and paprika. Cook for about 4-6 minutes, stirring frequently.
6. Warm up the soft taco shells and fill with the Brussels sprouts and corn salsa, then serve.

Red Lentil Falafel Pita Sandwich Recipe

Ingredients

- 1 cup dry red lentils
- ½ onion, diced
- 3 garlic cloves, minced
- 1 cup chopped parsley

- 1 teaspoon coriander
- 1 ½ teaspoons cumin, divided
- 1 ½ teaspoons salt, divided
- 2 tablespoons flour
- 2 tablespoons oil
- ¼ cup tahini
- 1 lemon, juiced
- 4 pita breads
- 4 lettuce leaves
- ½ cup halved grape tomatoes
- ¼ cup pepperoncini
- 2 sliced Persian cucumbers

Cooking Directions

1. Add the lentils to a bowl, cover with water to soak for 1 hour, then drain.

2. Add the drained lentils, onion, garlic, parsley, coriander, 1 teaspoon cumin, and 1 teaspoon salt to a food processor and blend until all the lentils are broken down.

3. Transfer to a bowl and stir in the flour.

4. Form the mixture into 16-18 small patties.

5. Add the oil to a large frying pan and bring the heat to medium.

6. Cook the falafel for about 8 minutes on each side until browned. You may have to work in batches.

7. In a small bowl combine the tahini, lemon juice, 3 tablespoons water, remaining ½ teaspoon

Kaitlyn Jones, RDN

cumin, and remaining ½ teaspoon salt.

8. Slice the pita bread in half and stuff the pocket with the falafel, lettuce, grape tomatoes, pepperoncini, cucumber, and tahini sauce.

9. Serve the red lentil falafel sandwiches.

Polos Curry (Sri Lankan Jackfruit Coconut Curry) Recipe

Ingredients

- 1 teaspoon mustard seeds
- 1 teaspoon cumin seeds
- 1 teaspoon coriander seeds
- 4 cardamom pods
- 1 cinnamon stick
- 10 curry leaves, dried or fresh
- 2 tablespoons coconut oil
- 1 large green chili, sliced (adjust to desired heat level)
- 2 shallots, diced
- 4 cloves garlic, minced
- 1 tablespoon grated ginger
- 1 teaspoon turmeric powder
- 1 (20-ounce) can green jackfruit, drained and shredded
- 1 (13.5-ounce) can coconut milk
- Salt, to taste

Cooking Directions

1. In a small pan, dry roast the mustard seeds, cumin seeds, coriander seeds, cardamom pods, cinnamon stick, and the curry leaves until fragrant.

2. Remove from the heat and coarsely grind.

3. Heat coconut oil in a large pan or pot over medium heat. Add the sliced green chilies and the roasted spice mixture. Saute for 1 minute.

4. Add the diced shallot and saute until translucent, about 3-4 minutes.

5. Add the minced garlic and grated ginger. Saute for 1 minute.

6. Stir in the turmeric powder and salt. Cook for 1 minute.

7. Add the shredded jackfruit and coconut milk. Bring to a simmer.

8. Reduce the heat to low, cover, and simmer for 15-20 minutes, stirring occasionally, until the jackfruit is tender and the curry has thickened.

9. Adjust seasoning with salt if needed and serve hot with rice or roti, if desired.

Baked Ratatouille Casserole With Garam Masala Recipe

Ingredients

- 1 small Chinese eggplant, cut into ½-inch pieces

- 1 small zucchini, chopped, cut into ½-inch pieces
- 1 small red bell pepper, cut into ½-inch pieces
- 1 small yellow or red onion, cut into ½-inch pieces
- 2 garlic cloves, minced (about 1 tablespoon)
- 1 (½-inch) piece ginger, minced (about 1 tablespoon)
- 2 tablespoons vegetable oil
- 1 ½ tablespoons Garam masala
- 2 teaspoons salt, divided
- 1 (14-ounce) can diced tomatoes
- 1 (14-ounce) can chickpeas
- ¼ cup chopped cilantro
- 1 lemon, cut into wedges

Cooking Directions

1. Preheat the oven to 400 F.
2. Add eggplant, zucchini, bell pepper, onion, garlic, and ginger to a 9x11-inch baking dish.
3. Toss with oil, Garam masala, and 1 teaspoon salt.
4. Bake for 30 minutes, stirring halfway through until the veggies shrink and soften.
5. Remove the baking dish from the oven and stir in tomatoes, chickpeas and their liquid, and 1 teaspoon salt

6. Bake for 30 minutes, stirring halfway through until the sauce is slightly thickened.

7. Remove from the oven and garnish with cilantro and lemon juice.

8. Serve the ratatouille with rice or naan.

Classic Kung Pao Tofu Recipe

Ingredients

- 1 (12-ounce) block extra firm tofu
- 3 tablespoons soy sauce
- 2 tablespoons Shaoxing wine
- 1 tablespoon rice vinegar
- 1 tablespoon plus 2 teaspoons cornstarch, divided
- 1 teaspoon sugar
- 4 tablespoons avocado oil, divided
- 4 cloves minced garlic
- 1 tablespoon minced ginger
- 1 teaspoon Sichuan peppercorns
- 4 dried whole Chinese chiles
- ½ cup dry roasted peanuts
- 5 scallions, diced

Optional Ingredients

- Steamed white rice, for serving

Cooking Directions

1. Wrap the tofu in a paper towel and place it on a cutting board.

2. Place a heavy sandwich press or pan on top of the tofu for 30 minutes to draw out any extra moisture.

3. While the tofu is resting, prepare the sauce by adding soy sauce, wine, vinegar, 2 teaspoons cornstarch, and sugar to a small bowl.

4. Whisk and set aside.

5. Cut the tofu into 1-inch cubes.

6. Transfer the tofu to a large bowl and toss to coat it with the remaining tablespoon of cornstarch.

7. Heat 2 tablespoons of oil in a wok over medium-high heat.

8. Working in two batches, brown the tofu on each side, approximately 6 minutes per batch.

9. Remove the tofu from the pan and place it on a paper towel.

10. Add the remaining 2 tablespoons of oil to the wok.

11. Add the garlic, ginger, peppercorns, and chiles to the wok. Stir and cook for 1 minute, until fragrant.

12. Add the sauce, peanuts, and scallions and stir to combine.

13. Add the tofu and stir fry for 2 minutes.

14. Serve the kung pao tofu with steamed rice, if desired.

Spaghetti And Zucchini Noodle Vegan Garden Pasta Recipe

Ingredients

- 6 cups halved cherry tomatoes
- 2 tablespoons olive oil, divided
- 4 minced garlic cloves, divided
- 1 teaspoon dried basil
- 1 teaspoon salt, divided
- 1 medium zucchini
- 1 diced shallot
- 8 ounces spaghetti
- 2 cups red chard, destemmed and chopped
- ¼ cup fresh basil

Cooking Directions

1. In a large bowl combine the tomatoes, 1 tablespoon of olive oil, 2 minced garlic cloves, dried basil, and ½ teaspoon of salt.

2. Cover and marinate on the counter for 1 hour.

3. When the tomatoes are done marinating, bring a large pot of water to boil.

4. While you wait for the water to boil, spiralize the zucchini.

5. Add the remaining oil to a large pan over medium heat.

6. Saute the shallots and remaining garlic for 5 minutes.

7. Add the spaghetti to the pot of boiling water and cook per package instructions.

8. When there is 1 minute left of cooking time for the spaghetti, add in the zucchini noodles.

9. Drain both the spaghetti and zucchini noodles in a colander.

10. Add both noodles to the frying pan with the shallots and garlic.

11. Stir in the tomatoes and red chard. Cover and cook on low for 10 minutes, stirring frequently.

12. Top with fresh basil and serve.

Twice-Fried Salt And Pepper Tofu Recipe

Ingredients

- 1 tablespoon Shaoxing wine
- 1 teaspoon sesame oil
- 1-inch knob fresh ginger, grated
- 1 grated + 4 chopped cloves garlic, divided
- 1 tablespoon + 1 teaspoon salt, divided
- 1 block firm tofu, drained and cut into 1-inch cubes
- ¼ cup cornstarch
- ¼ cup cornmeal
- ½ cup flour
- 1 tablespoon ground white pepper
- ¼ cup vegetable oil

- 2 green chiles, such as serrano, finely chopped
- 2 scallions, finely chopped

Cooking Directions

1. In a saucepan, combine 1 cup water, wine, sesame oil, grated ginger, 1 grated garlic clove, and 1 tablespoon salt. Bring to a boil.

2. Remove from the heat and add the tofu cubes. Brine for 15 minutes.

3. Transfer tofu to a paper towel–lined tray to drain until completely dry, about 15 minutes.

4. In a large bowl, combine cornstarch, cornmeal, flour, the remaining 1 teaspoon salt, and white pepper.

5. Add tofu and toss to coat.

6. Add oil to a wok and place over medium heat.

7. Once hot, add tofu and fry until golden brown, about 3–4 minutes per side.

8. Remove tofu from the wok and drain on a paper towel–lined plate.

9. Add chiles, scallions, and the remaining 4 chopped garlic cloves to the wok. Saute until fragrant, about 1 minute.

10. Return the tofu to the wok and fry with the aromatics until the garlic is golden, about 1–2 minutes. Do not burn the garlic.

11. Remove from the wok and serve immediately.

Silken Tofu And Soba Noodle Salad Recipe

Ingredients

- Juice of 1 lime, plus more for serving
- 1 tablespoon sesame oil
- 1 tablespoon soy sauce
- ¼ teaspoon red chili flakes
- 12 ounces silken tofu
- 6 ounces soba noodles
- ½ English cucumber, julienned
- ½ carrot, julienned
- 3 green onions, sliced
- ½ cup raw, unsalted cashews

Optional Ingredients

- fresh mint

Cooking Directions

1. In a small bowl combine the lime juice, sesame oil, soy sauce, and red chili flakes.
2. Cut the tofu into 1-inches cubes.
3. Pour the lime juice mixture over the tofu and marinate for 1 hour.
4. Cook the soba noodles according to the package instructions.
5. When the noodles are done cooking, drain and rinse under cold water.

6. Add the cashews to a dry skillet and toast on medium heat for 5-8 minutes, shaking the pan frequently.

7. To a large bowl, add the noodles, marinated tofu (along with the extra marinade in the bowl), cucumber, carrots, green onions, and toasted cashews.

8. Serve, optionally garnished with fresh mint and extra lime juice.

Sigeumchi Namul-Inspired Vegan Quiche Recipe

Ingredients

- For the crust

- 2 cups (250 grams) unbleached all-purpose flour

- 2 teaspoons granulated sugar

- ½ teaspoon kosher salt

- 1 scant cup (150 grams) refined coconut oil, room temperature (not liquid)

- 6 tablespoons ice-cold water, plus more as needed

- For the filling

- 14 ounces firm or extra-firm tofu

- 2 tablespoons soy milk

- 2 tablespoons nutritional yeast

- 2 teaspoons soy sauce

- 1 tablespoon gochujang paste

- 1 tablespoon sesame oil
- 1 tablespoon corn starch
- 1 clove garlic
- ¼ teaspoon turmeric
- 1 (10-ounce) package frozen chopped spinach, defrosted and squeezed free of water
- For the garnish
- 4 tablespoons gochujang paste
- ½ teaspoon sesame seeds
- 1 scallion, thinly sliced

Cooking Directions

1. Make the crust: Add the flour, sugar, and salt to a large mixing bowl and whisk to combine.
2. Add dollops of coconut oil to the dry mixture
3. Use your fingers to rub it in until it resembles coarse breadcrumbs.
4. Add the water 1 tablespoon at a time to form a soft but not sticky dough.
5. Transfer to a well-floured surface and form into a disc with your hands.
6. Flour the top of the dough and rolling pin and roll into a circle about 12 inches in diameter.
7. Fold the dough in half and transfer to a 9-inch pie plate.
8. Tuck the overhang under itself and crimp the dough around the edge of the plate.

9. Refrigerate the dough-lined plate until firm, about 30 minutes.

10. Adjust the oven rack to middle position and preheat the oven to 350 F.

11. Make the filling: Add all the filling ingredients except the spinach to the bowl of a food processor.

12. Process until well blended and smooth.

13. Transfer the filling to a mixing bowl and stir in the thawed spinach.

14. Pour the filling into the prepared pie plate.

15. Place in the oven and bake, uncovered, for 40 minutes, until firm and golden on top.

16. Meanwhile, place gochujang in the corner of a plastic bag and snip off the corner with scissors.

17. Pipe gochujang paste onto the cooked quiche and sprinkle with sesame seeds and scallions.

18. Slice and serve.

Super Springy Vegetable Soup Recipe

Ingredients

- 2 tablespoons oil
- 2 leeks, chopped
- 3 garlic cloves, minced
- 2 celery stalks, sliced
- 1 bunch asparagus, chopped
- 1 teaspoon salt

- ½ teaspoon black pepper
- 7 cups vegetable broth
- ¾ cup ditalini, or other small pasta
- 1 cup peas
- 4 cups chopped kale, no stems
- ½ cup chopped parsley
- ¼ cups chopped dill
- 1 (15-ounce) can white beans, drained
- ½ lemon, juiced

Optional Ingredients

- Chopped green onions

Cooking Directions

1. Add the oil to a soup pot and bring the heat to medium.
2. Add the leeks and cook for 5 minutes.
3. Add the garlic, celery, asparagus, salt, and pepper and cook for 3 more minutes.
4. Add the broth and pasta. Bring to a boil, then simmer for 15 minutes.
5. Add the peas, kale, parsley, dill, white beans, and lemon juice. Cook on low heat for 10 minutes, stirring frequently.
6. The soup is ready to serve. Garnish with chopped green onions, if desired.

Kaitlyn Jones, RDN

Cajun Tofu Bowl With Avocado-Maple Dressing Recipe

Ingredients

- 1 (16-ounce) package super firm tofu
- 4 tablespoons olive oil, divided
- 1 teaspoon paprika
- ½ teaspoon granulated garlic
- ½ teaspoon oregano
- ¼ teaspoon granulated onion
- ¼ teaspoon thyme
- ¼ teaspoon pepper and a pinch, divided
- ¼ teaspoon red pepper flakes
- ⅛ teaspoon cayenne
- 2 sliced red peppers
- 1 teaspoon salt and a pinch, divided
- 2 large avocados, divided
- ½ cup corn
- ½ cup diced tomatoes
- 1 tablespoon diced red onion
- 2 tablespoons apple cider vinegar, divided
- 2 tablespoons lime juice
- 2 tablespoons maple syrup
- ¼ cup cilantro
- 2 cups cooked rice

Cooking Directions

1. Preheat the oven to 400 F.
2. Cut the tofu into 1-inch cubes.

3. Put the cubed tofu in a bowl and mix with 1 tablespoon of the oil, paprika, granulated garlic, oregano, granulated onion, thyme, ¼ teaspoon of the pepper, red pepper flakes, and cayenne.

4. Lay the tofu on a baking sheet along with the red pepper slices. Drizzle the red peppers with 1 tablespoon of the oil and the pinch of salt and pepper. Bake for 30 minutes.

5. Cut one of the avocados and add to a bowl with the corn, diced tomatoes, and red onion.

6. Add 1 tablespoon of the olive oil, 1 tablespoon of the vinegar, and a ½ teaspoon of the salt to the avocado mixture and toss.

7. Add the remaining avocado, remaining tablespoon of oil, lime juice, remaining tablespoon of vinegar, remaining ½ teaspoon of salt, maple syrup, cilantro, and ¼ cup water to a blender and blend until smooth.

8. To assemble, add rice, tofu, red peppers, and avocado mixture to 2 bowls and top with the avocado maple dressing.

9. Serve the assembled bowls.

Kaitlyn Jones, RDN

Ethiopian-Inspired Berbere Split Peas Recipe

Ingredients

- ½ teaspoon whole black peppercorns
- ¼ teaspoon whole coriander seeds
- ¼ teaspoon whole cumin seeds
- 4 whole cloves
- 4 whole allspice berries
- 3 whole cardamom pods
- ¼ cup olive oil
- 1 large yellow onion, chopped
- 4 medium carrots, sliced
- 1 pound potatoes, cut into ½-inch cubes
- 4 garlic cloves, minced
- 2 inches ginger root, peeled and grated
- 1 tablespoon ground cayenne pepper (or less, to taste)
- 1 tablespoon ground sweet paprika
- 1 teaspoon ground turmeric
- ⅛ teaspoon ground cinnamon
- ⅛ teaspoon ground nutmeg
- 1 pound green split peas
- 1 teaspoon salt, or to taste

Optional Ingredients

- Lemon juice
- Injera bread
- Rice

Cooking Directions

1. Place the peppercorns, coriander, cumin, cloves, allspice, and cardamom in a dry frying pan, preferably cast-iron, and heat it on a medium flame.

2. Let toast for 3–4 minutes, shaking the pan periodically to prevent burning, until the spices are fragrant and slightly browned.

3. Remove from the heat and transfer the spices to a mortar. Grind the spices to a powder with the pestle, removing the cardamom pods as soon as they've broken open. Set aside.

4. Heat the oil in a large saucepan on medium heat.

5. Add the onion, carrots, and potatoes and saute, stirring occasionally, for 6–7 minutes.

6. Add the garlic and ginger and cook for 2 more minutes.

7. Transfer the ground spices from the mortar to the pan, and then add the cayenne pepper, paprika, turmeric, cinnamon, and nutmeg. Stir well and cook for 1 minute.

8. Add the split peas and 4 ½ cups of water, stir, and bring to a boil.

9. Lower the heat and let simmer, uncovered. Cook, stirring occasionally, for 40–45 minutes, or until the peas are tender, start to fall apart, and form a creamy mixture.

10. Stir in the salt and taste, adjusting for salt if necessary.
11. Serve immediately with an optional squeeze of lemon juice and with injera bread or rice, if desired.

Spicy Sriracha Tofu Spring Rolls Recipe

Ingredients

- 8 ounces super firm tofu
- 1 tablespoon + 1 teaspoon avocado oil, divided
- 5 tablespoons soy sauce, divided
- 4 tablespoons sriracha, divided
- ¼ teaspoon seasoned sriracha powder
- 2 ounces rice noodles
- ½ cup peanut butter
- 1 tablespoon maple syrup
- 2 tablespoons lime juice
- 2 carrots, cut into thin strips
- 1 English cucumber, cut into thin strips
- 4 kale leaves, destemmed
- 12 rice paper wrappers

Cooking Directions

1. Cut the tofu into long, thin strips, about ¼-inch thick.
2. In a small bowl combine 1 teaspoon of avocado oil, 3

tablespoons of soy sauce, 2 tablespoons of sriracha, and the sriracha powder.

3. Add the tofu strips and marinade to a shallow container and let sit for 30 minutes.

4. Cook the rice noodles and drain according to package Cooking Directions. Set aside.

5. Add the remaining 1 tablespoon of avocado oil to a frying pan over medium heat.

6. Add the tofu and cook for 15 minutes, stirring occasionally.

7. To make the sauce, combine the remaining soy sauce, peanut butter, maple syrup, remaining sriracha, lime juice, and ¼ cup water.

8. Pour warm water in a large frying pan big enough to accommodate the rice paper rounds.

9. Dip the rice paper into the water for 5 seconds then place on a work surface.

10. Assemble the spring roll by adding in a small amount of tofu strips, carrots, cucumber, kale, and rice noodles.

11. Wrap rice paper over the filling then fold in the sides and continue rolling. Repeat until all spring rolls are wrapped.

12. Serve the spicy sriracha tofu spring rolls with sauce.

Kaitlyn Jones, RDN

6

Recipes for Low Cholesterol Vegan Snacks and Desserts Diet

Vegan Chocolate-Covered Digestive Biscuits (Vegan McVities)

Ingredients

- 4 1/2 ounces all-purpose flour (about 1 cup, spooned; 125g)

- 2 ounces whole wheat flour (about 1/3 cup; 55g), plus more for dusting

- 2 1/4 ounces quick-toasted sugar (about 1/3 cup; 60g)

- 1/2 teaspoon cream of tartar

- 1/4 teaspoon baking powder

- 1/4 teaspoon baking soda

- 1/8 teaspoon (0.5g) Diamond Crystal kosher salt; for table salt, use about half as much by volume or use the same weight

- 4 ounces refined coconut oil (about 2/3 cup; 113g), solid and cool

- 3/4 ounce water (about 5 1/4 teaspoons; 20g)
- 9 ounces roughly chopped vegan chocolate (about 1 1/2 cups; 285g) (see note)

Cooking Directions

1. **Make the Dough:** Adjust oven rack to lower-middle position and preheat to 350°F (175°C). Combine all-purpose flour, whole wheat flour, toasted sugar, cream of tartar, baking powder, baking soda, salt, and solid coconut oil in the bowl of a food processor. Process until oil virtually disappears into a fine, floury meal. Add water and pulse to form a damp and crumbly dough. Turn onto an unfloured surface and knead into a ball.

2. **Roll and Bake the Biscuits:** On a generously floured surface, roll dough until just shy of 1/4 inch (4.7mm), using as much flour as needed along the way to prevent sticking. Dust away excess flour with a pastry brush and decorate with a docking tool if you like. Cut into 2 3/4-inch rounds and transfer to a parchment-lined half sheet pan. Gather up scraps, knead, roll, and cut as before.

3. Bake until firm and dry to the touch but quite pale, about 22 minutes. Cool directly on sheet pan and continue with next step, or store in an airtight container up

to 3 days at room temperature.

4. **Temper the Chocolate:** Temper chocolate according to one of the methods described here.

5. **Coat the Biscuits:** Working with just 2 or 3 biscuits at a time, dollop a generous 1/2 tablespoon, or just over 1/4 ounce, chocolate over each. Spread into an even layer over biscuit and, as chocolate starts to thicken, bounce the tines of a fork across the surface to create a wavy pattern. Repeat with remaining biscuits and chocolate. (Before it hardens, store excess chocolate.) Serve biscuits immediately, preferably with hot tea, and transfer to an airtight container for up to 3 weeks at room temperature.

Homemade Wheat Thins Recipe

Ingredients

For the Glaze:

- 2 ounces light corn syrup (about 3 tablespoons; 55g)

- 1/4 ounce barley malt syrup (about 1 1/2 teaspoons; 7g)

- 1/4 teaspoon (1g) Diamond Crystal kosher salt; for table salt, use half as much by volume or use the same weight

- 1 ounce hot water (about 2 tablespoons; 30g)

Kaitlyn Jones, RDN

For the Crackers:

- 5 ounces whole wheat flour, plus more for dusting (about 1 cup, spooned; 140g)
- 2 1/2 ounces sugar (about 1/3 cup; 70g)
- 1 1/2 ounces bread flour (about 1/4 cup, spooned; 40g)
- 3/4 ounce toasted wheat germ (about 3 tablespoons; 20g)
- 1/2 teaspoon ground turmeric
- 1/2 teaspoon (2g) Diamond Crystal kosher salt, plus more for sprinkling; for table salt, use half as much by volume or use the same weight
- 1/2 teaspoon cream of tartar
- 1/4 teaspoon baking soda
- 1 ounce refined coconut oil, solid but creamy (about 2 tablespoons; 30g)
- 1/4 ounce barley malt syrup (1 1/2 teaspoons; 7g)
- 3 ounces water (about 1/3 cup plus 1 tablespoon; 85g)

Cooking Directions

1. **For the Glaze:** Combine corn syrup, malted barley syrup, and salt in a small bowl, then add hot water and stir with a fork until the salt is dissolved. Set aside to cool.

2. **For the Crackers:** Adjust oven rack to lower-middle position, preheat to 350°F, and cut two

parchment sheets to 11- by 16-inches. Combine whole wheat flour, sugar, bread flour, wheat germ, salt, turmeric, cream of tartar, baking soda, and coconut oil in the bowl of a food processor. Pulse until coconut oil disappears into a fine, powdery meal. Mix barley malt and water in a small glass to dissolve the syrup, then add to dry mix and process to form a stiff dough. Knead lightly on an unfloured surface, then divide in half and drape with a damp paper towel.

3. **To Roll:** Place a prepared parchment sheet on a clean work surface, and dust generously with whole wheat flour. Place one portion of dough in the center, sprinkle with flour, and, using a rolling pin, roll into a roughly 5- by 8-inch rectangle. Dust with flour and carefully flip the dough over, sprinkling more flour on top, wherever you notice a sticky patch. Continue rolling from the center out, until the dough extends just past the edges of the parchment and is no thicker than 1/16 inch; the crackers will puff significantly in the oven, so this thinness is key to keeping them thin and crisp.

4. **To Glaze and Cut:** Trim away the ragged edges with a pizza wheel, and lightly brush the dough with glaze. If you like, use a docking tool to decorate the crackers. Cut into 1 1/2-inch squares with a pizza wheel (they

will shrink in the oven), then carefully transfer the parchment and crackers to an aluminum half sheet pan. This can be done by lifting two opposite corners and pulling the paper taut, or by sliding the parchment and crackers on and off a pizza peel.

5. **To Bake:** Sprinkle with salt and bake the crackers to a light yellow-brown, about 12 minutes, rotating the sheet pan halfway through to ensure even browning in the ultra-thin dough. The bake-time is *highly variable*, depending on the exact thickness of the dough, the type of baking sheet used, and any variations in dough thickness. Keep a close eye on the crackers as they bake, as they may brown and crisp faster depending on these variables. Cool to room temperature directly on the baking sheet; the crackers will not be crisp while warm. Repeat with the remaining dough (if rolled/cut in advance, the crackers won't shrink away from each other as they should). Store leftovers in an airtight container at room temperature up to one month.

Vegan Spinach and Artichoke Dip Recipe

Ingredients

- 1 cup (235ml) homemade vegetable stock or low-sodium vegetable broth

- 1 pound (450g) cauliflower, cored and cut into medium florets (12 ounces; 340g after prep)
- 2 ounces raw cashews (55g; 1/2 cup)
- 1/4 cup (60ml) homemade or store-bought vegan mayonnaise
- 2 tablespoons nutritional yeast
- 1 tablespoon (15ml) Dijon mustard
- 1 tablespoon (15ml) fresh lemon juice
- 2 teaspoons garlic powder
- Kosher salt
- 2 large cloves garlic, minced

- 2 tablespoons (30ml) extra-virgin olive oil
- 1 (10-ounce; 285g) box frozen spinach, thawed and squeezed of excess liquid, or 12 ounces fresh spinach, trimmed or 10 ounces (340g) fresh baby spinach
- 1 (14-ounce; 395g) can artichokes, artichokes drained and halved
- Freshly ground black pepper
- Tortilla chips or pita chips, for serving

Cooking Directions

1. Preheat the oven to 350°F (177°C). In a large deep skillet, bring vegetable stock to a simmer over medium heat. Add cashews and cauliflower and stir to

coat, then reduce the heat to medium low. Cover and cook until the cauliflower is very tender when pierced with a knife, about 10 minutes. (If the broth seems to be steaming from the lid, reduce the heat to low. You want to cook the cauliflower while retaining as much of the liquid as possible.)

2. Transfer the cauliflower, cashews, and liquid to a food processor and let cool for 1 minute. Purée until very smooth. (You need to keep the machine running for a minute or more, scraping down the sides periodically, to get a super smooth purée.)

3. Add mayonnaise, nutritional yeast, mustard, lemon juice, garlic powder, and process until incorporated. Season with salt.

4. Wipe out the skillet. Add olive oil and heat over medium heat until warmed. Add minced garlic and cook, stirring, until fragrant and softened, 1 to 2 minutes. Add spinach, a large pinch of salt, and cook, stirring, until wilted, if fresh, or heated through, if frozen. Transfer spinach to a fine-mesh strainer and press or squeeze to drain any excess liquid.

5. Add cooked spinach and artichokes to the food processor and pulse a few times, just until incorporated. Taste and season with salt and pepper.

6. Scrape the dip into a 1-quart baking dish and bake for about 30 minutes, until just starting to brown around the edges. To brown the top, turn on the broiler and arrange the pan within 4 inches of the heat. Broil until the dip is browned to your liking, 2 to 3 minutes. (If you're in a rush, you can skip the baking step and just serve the dip while it's warm or room temperature, right from the food processor. Alternatively, you can make the dip a day ahead and bake it the following day. Just add 10 minutes to the cooking time.)

7. Serve hot with chips.

Potato Chips With Mushrooms, Lemon, and Thyme Recipe

Ingredients

- 3 tablespoons nutritional yeast
- 1/4 ounce dried mushrooms, such as cremini
- 1/4 teaspoon finely grated zest from 1 lemon
- 1/4 teaspoon granulated garlic
- 1 teaspoon minced fresh thyme or 1/2 teaspoon crushed dried thyme
- 1 recipe Extra-Crunchy Potato Chips
- Kosher salt and freshly ground black pepper

Cooking Directions

1. In an electric spice grinder or high-power blender, combine nutritional yeast, dried mushrooms, lemon zest, garlic powder, and thyme and blend until a fine powder forms.

2. While chips are still hot and fresh from the oil, and working in batches if necessary, set in a large paper-towel-lined bowl and sprinkle nutritional yeast mixture all over. Season with salt and pepper. Using clean hands, toss to coat chips evenly, then transfer to a serving bowl. Cooled chips can be stored in a zipper-lock bag or airtight container for up to 2 days.

Za'atar (Thyme-, Sesame-, and Sumac-Spiced) Popcorn Recipe

Ingredients

- 1/2 cup popcorn kernels, popped (about 8 cups popped)

- 4 tablespoons extra-virgin olive oil

- 1/4 cup store-bought za'atar spice blend (available at specialty food stores and Amazon)

- Kosher salt

Cooking Directions

1. Place popped popcorn in a large mixing bowl and drizzle olive all

over, tossing to coat evenly. Add za'atar, tossing to coat evenly. Season with salt and serve. Popcorn can be stored at room temperature in a zipper-lock bag overnight.

Cheese-Free Sweet Potato "Quesadillas" Recipe

Ingredients

- 1 large sweet potato (about 12 ounces; 340g)

- Small handful minced fresh cilantro leaves (see notes)

- 3 tablespoons (45g) minced pickled jalapeños (see notes)

- 3 scallions, thinly sliced (see notes)

- Kosher salt

- 4 to 6 (8-inch) flour tortillas

- Vegetable oil, as needed

Cooking Directions

1. Preheat oven to 425°F (220°C). Place sweet potato in an oven-safe vessel (such as a cast iron pan or a small baking dish) and roast until a knife or skewer inserted into its center meets no resistance, about 40 minutes. Remove from oven and allow to cool. Roasted sweet potato can be wrapped and stored in refrigerator for several days before you continue with the recipe.

2. Peel and discard sweet potato skin and mash flesh with a fork in a medium bowl. Add cilantro, pickled jalapeños, and scallions (see notes). Stir and fold to combine. Season to taste with salt.

3. Spread about 1/2 cup of the mixture evenly over half of 1 tortilla, leaving a 1/2-inch border. Fold tortilla over and seal edges by pressing down firmly. Repeat with remaining filling and as many tortillas as needed (about 4 to 6, depending on the exact size of the sweet potato).

4. Heat 2 tablespoons (30ml) oil in a large skillet or on a griddle over medium heat until shimmering. Carefully add 2 folded tortillas and cook, swirling and moving tortillas around, until golden brown and puffy on first side, about 2 minutes. Using a flexible metal spatula, flip quesadillas, season with salt, and continue cooking until golden brown and puffy on second side, about 2 minutes longer.

5. Transfer quesadillas to a paper towel to drain and repeat step 4 to cook remaining quesadillas. Serve immediately.

Oven-Roasted Tomato Bruschetta Recipe

Ingredients

- 2 (28-ounce; 794g) cans peeled whole tomatoes, drained, stem ends trimmed and any bits of skin removed
- Kosher salt
- 1/4 cup (60ml) extra-virgin olive oil, plus more for drizzling
- 15 large basil leaves, thinly sliced into a chiffonade
- Red wine vinegar, to taste
- Sugar, to taste
- Freshly toasted sliced bread, for serving
- Halved garlic cloves, for rubbing on toasts

Cooking Directions

1. Preheat oven to 300°F (150°C). Line a rimmed baking sheet with parchment paper. Working over a bowl, using your fingers, tear each tomato in half and press out and discard the seeds. Arrange tomatoes on prepared baking sheet in one layer, season with salt, and drizzle all over with olive oil. Transfer to oven and cook until excess juices have evaporated and tomatoes look slightly dry on the exterior but still moist within, about 1 hour.

2. Transfer oven-roasted tomatoes to a work surface and chop finely.

3. Transfer to a large mixing bowl. Add 1/4 cup olive oil and basil

and stir well. Season with salt and add red wine vinegar, about 1 teaspoon at a time, until tomatoes are very lightly tart. Stir in a pinch of sugar to help pump up tomatoes' natural sweetness even more; add more sugar sparingly to taste, if desired.

4. Rub top sides of toasts all over with garlic (rub more on for a stronger flavor, or less for a gentler one). Drizzle toasts with olive oil and season lightly with salt. Spoon tomatoes on top and serve.

Oven-Dried Grapes (a.k.a. Raisins) Recipe

Ingredients

- 3 large bunches seedless grapes, preferably mixed colors, stemmed

- Vegetable or canola oil, for greasing

Cooking Directions

1. Preheat oven to 225°F (110°C). Very lightly grease 2 rimmed baking sheets with oil, then scatter grapes all over. Bake, checking periodically for doneness, until grapes are nicely shriveled and semi-dried but still slightly plump, about 4 hours (see note). (The exact time will depend on your grapes, your oven, and your preferred degree

of dryness.) Let cool. Use a thin metal spatula to free any grapes that are stuck to the baking sheet.

2. The dried grapes can be refrigerated in a sealed container for about 3 weeks. (How long they keep will also depend on their degree of dryness; drier grapes will keep longer.)

Notes

The precise cooking time can vary quite a bit depending on the size of your grapes (larger ones will take longer to dry than smaller ones) and how your oven functions (some ovens are prone to big temperature swings, which can speed up and/or slow down total drying time). Make sure to check in on the progress of your grapes periodically to avoid any mishaps.

Avocado Toast With Radishes, Baby Peas, and Fresh Herbs Recipe

Ingredients

- 1 slice country or sandwich bread, approximately 1/2 inch thick

- Extra-virgin olive oil

- 1/2 medium pitted and peeled Hass avocado

- Small handful baby peas (see note), or enough to lightly cover surface of bread

- 6 thin slices radish from 1 to 2 radishes, or enough to cover surface of bread

Kaitlyn Jones, RDN

- Freshly squeezed lemon juice to taste, from 1/2 lemon

- Finely chopped basil leaves, for garnish

- Kosher salt and freshly ground black pepper

Cooking Directions

1. Lightly brush bread with olive oil and toast to desired level of doneness. Top with avocado and mash with a fork to cover entire surface. Add peas, pressing gently to anchor them in avocado. Top with radish slices. Squeeze lemon juice over surface and sprinkle with basil, salt, and pepper. Serve.

Notes

The volume of each ingredient will depend on the size of your bread and personal preference. Apply to taste. If you cannot find fresh peas, frozen baby peas are a great substitute. Bring to room temperature under cool running water.

The Best Applesauce

Ingredients

- 4 pounds mixed apples (about 12 medium apples; 1.8kg)

- 3 1/2 ounces plain or toasted sugar (about 1/2 cup; 100g)

- 1/2 teaspoon (2g) Diamond Crystal kosher salt; for table salt, use about half as much by volume or the same weight

- 1 ounce apple cider vinegar (about 2 tablespoons; 30g)

- 1 (3-inch) strip orange peel

- 1 (3-inch) cinnamon stick

- Apple cider, to adjust consistency

- 1/4 teaspoon rose water (optional)

Cooking Directions

1. Core apples without peeling, then slice and roughly chop into 1/2- to 1/4-inch pieces. This will yield approximately 3 1/2 pounds prepared fruit (16 cups; 1.5kg). Transfer to a 5-quart Dutch oven, along with sugar, salt, apple cider vinegar, orange peel, and cinnamon stick. Stir to combine, then cover and place over medium heat until apples have wilted and begun to bubble in their own juices, about 15 minutes. If this process seems to be moving slowly, simply turn up the heat.

2. Continue cooking, stirring from time to time, until apples are fall-apart tender, about 10 minutes more. Remove orange peel and cinnamon stick, then purée to your desired consistency with an immersion blender or food processor (see notes). If desired, thin as needed with apple cider to adjust consistency. For a more intense apple flavor, season with 1/4 teaspoon rose water.

3. Transfer applesauce to glass jars and

refrigerate up to 3 weeks. If freezing, make certain not to overfill the containers, as the applesauce will expand once frozen.

Easy Vegan Crispy Tofu Spring Rolls

Ingredients

- 1 (14-ounce; 400g) block firm (non-silken) tofu, cut into matchsticks approximately 2 inches long and 1/2 inch square
- 3 tablespoons (45ml) vegetable oil
- 1 recipe peanut-tamarind dipping sauce
- 1 large carrot, peeled and cut into a fine julienne
- 4 ounces pea greens
- 2 cups mixed picked fresh herbs, such as cilantro, mint, and Thai basil
- Chopped toasted peanuts
- Finely sliced Thai bird or serrano chile peppers
- 20 dried spring roll rice paper wrappers

Cooking Directions

1. Place tofu in a large colander and set in the sink. Pour 1 quart boiling water over tofu and let rest for 1 minute. Transfer to a paper towel–lined tray and press dry. Heat vegetable oil in a large nonstick or cast iron

skillet over medium-low heat until shimmering. Add tofu and cook, turning occasionally, until golden brown and crisp on all surfaces, about 10 minutes total. Transfer to a paper towel–lined plate to drain.

2. Transfer drained tofu to a large bowl and add 5 tablespoons peanut-tamarind sauce. Toss to coat tofu.

3. Transfer tofu, carrots, greens, herbs, peanuts, peppers, and remaining dipping sauce to serving platters. Serve with rice paper wrappers and a bowl of warm water. To eat, dip a rice paper wrapper in warm water until moist on all surfaces, then transfer to your plate. Place a small amount of desired fillings in the center. Roll the front edge of the wrapper over the filling away from you, then fold the right side over toward the center. Continue rolling until a tight roll with one open end has formed. Dip spring roll in dipping sauce as you eat.

Korean Fried Cauliflower (Vegan) Recipe

Ingredients

- 2 quarts vegetable or peanut oil
- 1/2 cup cornstarch
- 1/2 cup all-purpose flour

- 1/2 teaspoon baking powder
- 1/3 cup toasted sesame seeds, plus more for garnish
- 1/3 cup unsweetened coconut flakes
- Kosher salt
- 1/2 cup cold water
- 1/2 cup vodka
- 1 head cauliflower, cut into 1-inch florets
- 1 recipe Sweet Soy Sauce or Sweet and Spicy Chili Sauce
- 4 to 5 finely sliced scallions

Cooking Directions

1. Preheat oil to 350°F in a large wok, Dutch oven, or deep fryer.

2. Combine cornstarch, flour, baking powder, 2 teaspoons kosher salt, sesame seeds, and coconut in a large bowl and whisk until homogenous. Add water and vodka and whisk until a smooth batter is formed, adding up to 2 tablespoons additional water if batter is too thick. It should have the consistency of thin paint and fall off of the whisk in thin ribbons that instantly disappear as they hit the surface of the batter in the bowl.

3. Add cauliflower to batter. Working one at a time, lift one piece and allow excess batter to drip off.

Carefully lower into hot oil. Repeat with remaining cauliflower until wok or fryer is full. Do not crowd pan. (You'll be able to fit about half of the cauliflower in each batch). Fry, using a metal spider or slotted spatula to rotate and agitate pieces as they cook until evenly golden brown and crisp all over, about 6 minutes. Transfer to a paper towel-lined plate and season immediately with salt. Keep warm while you fry the remaining cauliflower.

4. Toss fried cauliflower with sauce and serve immediately, sprinkled with extra sesame seeds and scallions.

Low Cholesterol Vegan Hummus

Ingredients

- 1/2 pound dried chickpeas (1 generous cup; 225g); see notes

- 2 teaspoons (12g) baking soda, divided

- Kosher salt

- 1 small onion, split in half

- 1 small stalk celery

- 1 small carrot

- 2 medium cloves garlic

- 2 bay leaves

- 1 1/2 cups (350ml) tahini sauce with garlic and lemon

- Extra-virgin olive oil, for serving

- Za'atar, paprika, warmed whole chickpeas, and/or chopped fresh parsley leaves, for serving

Cooking Directions

1. Combine beans, 1 teaspoon (6g) baking soda, and 2 tablespoons (24g) kosher salt in a large bowl and cover with 6 cups (1.4L) cold water. Stir to dissolve salt and baking soda. Let stand at room temperature overnight. Drain and rinse beans thoroughly.

2. Place beans in a large Dutch oven or saucepan. Add remaining baking soda, 1 tablespoon (12g) salt, onion, celery, carrot, garlic, and bay leaves.

Add 6 cups (1.4L) water and bring to a boil over high heat. Reduce to a simmer, cover with lid slightly cracked, and cook until beans are completely tender, to the point of falling apart, about 2 hours. Check on beans occasionally and top up with more water if necessary; they should be completely submerged at all times.

3. Discard onion, celery, and bay leaves. Transfer chickpeas, carrot, and garlic to a food processor or high-powered blender (such as a Vitamix, BlendTec, or Breville Boss; see note) with 1 cup (235ml) cooking liquid. Cover blender, taking out the central insert on the blender lid.

4. Place a folded kitchen towel over the hole in the center of the lid to allow steam to escape. Holding

the towel down firmly, turn the blender to the lowest possible speed and slowly increase speed to high. If the mixture becomes too thick to blend, add cooking liquid, 1/4 cup (60ml) at a time, until a very smooth, thick, and spreadable purée forms, always starting the blender on low speed before increasing to high. If your blender comes with a push-stick for thick purées, use it. Continue blending until completely smooth, about 2 minutes. Transfer 1 cup cooking liquid to an airtight container and refrigerate.

5. Transfer hot chickpea mixture to a large bowl. Whisk in tahini sauce. Whisk in salt to taste. Transfer to a sealed container and allow to cool to room temperature. It should thicken up until it can hold its shape when spooned onto a plate. If purée is too thick, add reserved cooking liquid, 1 tablespoon at a time, until hummus is desired consistency.

6. Serve hummus on a wide, shallow plate, drizzled with olive oil and sprinkled with za'atar, paprika, warmed whole chickpeas, and/or chopped parsley. Leftover hummus can be stored in the refrigerator for up to 1 week. Allow to come to room temperature before serving.

Kaitlyn Jones, RDN

7

Making This Diet Work for You

There's a lot of advice on eating healthy, but what if you could also eat sustainably—without sacrificing the foods you love? We've created an easy-to-follow sustainable diet guide to help you get started.

So what, exactly is a sustainable diet? It's a diet that's vibrant, delicious, and good for both your health and the planet. It focuses on local, seasonal, and plant-based ingredients, supports sustainable farming practices, and uses fewer resources.

The food you eat has a bigger environmental impact than you might think, but by adopting a sustainable eating plan, you can make a big difference. Your diet is a personal choice, but cooking sustainable meals can be both simple and delicious.

1. Eat More Plants

Fruits and vegetables are rich in essential nutrients that optimize our health and typically have a much lower environmental impact compared to meat, dairy, and processed foods. However, some exceptions exist, including fragile produce that is shipped thousands of miles, vegetables grown in protected conditions (like hothouse tomatoes), and resource-intensive foods like almonds and GMO soy. By eating more locally sourced, seasonal produce, you can maximize both health benefits and sustainability.

2. Eat More Variety

Our food choices are harming both our health and the planet: 75% of the global food supply comes from just 12 plant and 5 animal species. This lack of variety in our diets puts pressure on critical ecosystems and threatens global food security. To create a more nutritious, flavorful, and eco-friendly meal, try building colorful plates filled with a variety of whole foods. And don't be afraid to try unique, locally available ingredients!

3. Reduce Your Food Waste

One-fifth of the food that is produced for human consumption is lost or wasted globally. This loss and waste generates up to 10% of global greenhouse gas emissions—nearly five times that of the aviation sector. To help reduce waste, try buying only what you'll eat before it spoils, composting your scraps, and freezing or preserving anything you won't use immediately. There are also many other effective ways to reduce waste beyond just your diet!

4. Eat Less Animal Products

Raising livestock for human consumption generates around 15% of total global greenhouse gas emissions—more than all transportation emissions combined. Still feel like you **need** animal protein to feel your best? Try limiting your consumption of meat and dairy products to just a few days a week. Whenever possible, choose more sustainable options, such as sustainably produced chicken instead of beef, to reduce your environmental impact.

5. Eat Local and Eat Seasonally

Grow your own organic vegetables or support a local, sustainable farm. Choose in-season ingredients to reduce costs, as storing food beyond its growing season can be resource-intensive. By supporting local farmers, you not only benefit your health but also contribute to your local economy.

6. Avoid Processed Foods

Aside from being bad for your health, processed foods require a lot of resources, and lose most of their nutrients during production. Even brown rice, which is considered a healthier alternative to white rice, consumes large amounts of water. To make more sustainable and nutritious choices, buy whole, unprocessed foods like buckwheat, quinoa, wild rice, unrefined barley, and wheat berries.

7. Choose Sustainably Sourced Seafood

Seafood can be a healthy addition to your diet, but high demand and poor management have resulted in overfishing of popular species like North Sea cod and wild Atlantic salmon. To make more sustainable choices, explore alternatives such as barramundi, wild-caught sardines, or sustainably farmed shellfish. These options are not only delicious but also better for the environment.

8. Give Plant Proteins a Chance

Plant-based proteins, such as beans, pulses, and certain grains, are far less resource-intensive than animal proteins like beef and chicken. They are also heart-healthy and easier to digest. For a delicious, sustainable alternative, try swapping lentils for beef in dishes like tacos or shepherd's pie—it's a flavorful and filling option that you might just love!

9. Buy in Bulk

Proper food packaging, especially of meat and seafood, is critical for food safety. But when it is practical, opt for bulk items instead of individually packaged products, bring reusable shopping and bulk bags to the store, and choose products with sustainable packaging materials to help minimize waste

Made in the USA
Las Vegas, NV
09 May 2025